TYNDALE OLD COMMENTARIES

VOLUME 27

TOTC

NAHUM, HABAKKUK AND ZEPHANIAH

Dedicated to our grandchildren:
Steph Snyman
Marise Snyman
Anrike le Roux
Eugene le Roux
Lara van Zyl
Janke van Zyl
With sincere gratitude for the joy
you bring to us as grandparents.

Tyndale Old Testament Commentaries

Volume 27

Series Editor: David G. Firth
Consulting Editor: Tremper Longman III

Nahum, Habakkuk and Zephaniah

An Introduction and Commentary

S. D. Snyman

Academic
An imprint of InterVarsity Press
Downers Grove, Illinois

InterVarsity Press, USA
P.O. Box 1400
Downers Grove, IL 60515-1426, USA
ivpress.com
email@ivpress.com

Inter-Varsity Press, England
36 Causton Street
London SW1P 4ST, England
ivpbooks.com
ivp@ivpbooks.com

©2020 by S. D. Snyman

InterVarsity Press®, USA, is the book-publishing division of InterVarsity Christian Fellowship/USA® and a member movement of the International Fellowship of Evangelical Students. Website: intervarsity.org.

Inter-Varsity Press, England, originated within the Inter-Varsity Fellowship, now the Universities and Colleges Christian Fellowship, a student movement connecting Christian Unions in universities and colleges throughout Great Britain, and a member movement of the International Fellowship of Evangelical Students. That historic association is maintained, and all senior IVP staff and committee members subscribe to the UCCF Basis of Faith. Website: www.uccf.org.uk.

Unless otherwise stated, Scripture quotations are taken from the Holy Bible, New International Version (Anglicized edition). For Scripture acknowledgments, see page xii.

First published 2020

USA ISBN 978-0-8308-4275-9 (print)
USA ISBN 978-0-8308-5115-7 (digital)

UK ISBN 978-1-78359-974-5 (print)
UK ISBN 978-1-78359-975-2 (digital)

Set in Garamond 11/13pt

Typeset in Great Britain by CRB Associates, Potterhanworth, Lincolnshire

Printed in the United States of America ∞

InterVarsity Press is committed to ecological stewardship and to the conservation of natural resources in all our operations. This book was printed using sustainably sourced paper.

Library of Congress Cataloging-in-Publication Data
A catalog record for this book is available from the Library of Congress.

British Library Cataloguing in Publication Data
A catalogue record for this book is available from the British Library.

P	21	20	19	18	17	16	15	14	13	12	11	10	9	8	7	6	5	4	3	2	1
Y	37	36	35	34	33	32	31	30	29	28	27	26	25	24	23	22	21	20

CONTENTS

GENERAL PREFACE

The decision to completely revise the Tyndale Old Testament Commentaries is an indication of the important role that the series has played since its opening volumes were released in the mid-1960s. They represented at that time, and have continued to represent, commentary writing that was committed to both the importance of the text of the Bible as Scripture and a desire to engage with as full a range of interpretative issues as possible without being lost in the minutiae of scholarly debate. The commentaries aimed to explain the biblical text to a generation of readers confronting models of critical scholarship and new discoveries from the Ancient Near East while remembering that the Old Testament is not simply another text from the ancient world. Although no uniform process of exegesis was required, all the original contributors were united in their conviction that the Old Testament remains the word of God for us today. That the original volumes fulfilled this role is evident from the way in which they continue to be used in so many parts of the world.

A crucial element of the original series was that it should offer an up-to-date reading of the text, and it is precisely for this reason that new volumes are required. The questions confronting readers in the first half of the twenty-first century are not necessarily those from the second half of the twentieth. Discoveries from the Ancient Near East continue to shed new light on the Old Testament, while emphases in exegesis have changed markedly. While it remains true to the goals of the initial volumes, the need for contemporary study of the text requires that the series as a whole be updated. This updating is not simply a matter of commissioning new volumes to replace the old. We have also taken the opportunity to update the format of the series to reflect a key emphasis from linguistics, which is that texts communicate in larger blocks rather than in shorter segments such as individual verses. Because of this, the treatment of each section of the text includes three segments. First, a short note on *Context* is offered, placing the passage under consideration in its literary setting within the book as well as noting any historical issues crucial to interpretation. The *Comment* segment then follows the traditional structure of the commentary, offering exegesis of the various components of a passage. Finally, a brief comment is made on *Meaning*, by which is meant the message that the passage seeks to communicate within the book, highlighting its key theological themes. This section brings together the detail of the *Comment* to show how the passage under consideration seeks to communicate as a whole.

Our prayer is that these new volumes will continue the rich heritage of the Tyndale Old Testament Commentaries and that they will continue to witness to the God who is made known in the text.

David G. Firth, Series Editor
Tremper Longman III, Consulting Editor

AUTHOR'S PREFACE

It was a pleasant surprise when I was requested by the editors of Tyndale Old Testament Commentaries a couple of years ago to contribute a volume to this series. At the completion of this responsibility entrusted to me, I wish to thank them for giving me the privilege of writing this commentary. In particular I want to thank the editor and staff members involved in finalizing the manuscript, for their prompt responses, meaningful comments, meticulous attention to detail and the professional way in which the project was handled from their side. It has indeed been a privilege working with you.

I was granted special leave by the University of the Free State in Bloemfontein, South Africa, to write this commentary. I owe the university authorities and in particular Professor Corli Witthuhn (Vice Rector for Research) a word of sincere appreciation for the generous leave that was granted to me to complete the commentary on time. The staff members at the library services of the University of the Free State were also extremely helpful in searching for and obtaining the necessary literature on the books of Nahum, Habakkuk and Zephaniah. In this regard I want to mention Mrs Hesma van Tonder and thank her for the help she provided in finding relevant literature.

I also want to thank my wife, Estie, who had to endure a husband spending many hours in his study busy researching and writing this commentary.

I trust that this commentary will succeed in leading interested Bible readers, theological students, pastors, Old Testament scholars and theologians to the text of the different books and in opening up the theological message of these three (sometimes neglected) prophetic books in the Old Testament.

S. D. (Fanie) Snyman
Bloemfontein, South Africa

ABBREVIATIONS

BZAW   Beihefte zur Zeitschrift für die alttestamentliche
          Wissenschaft
COT   Commentaar op het Oude Testament
FOTL   Forms of the Old Testament Literature
HCOT   Historical Commentary on the Old Testament
HTS   *Hervormde Teologiese Studies*
IECOT   International Exegetical Commentary on the
          Old Testament
JSOTSup   Journal for the Study of the Old Testament:
          Supplement Series
KAT   Kommentar zum Alten Testament
KHAT   Kurzer Hand-Kommentar zum Alten Testament
LXX   Septuagint (pre-Christian Greek version of the
          Old Testament)
NIBC   New International Biblical Commentary on the
          Old Testament
NICOT   New International Commentary on the Old
          Testament
POT   De Prediking van het Oude Testament
SHBC   Smyth & Helwys Bible Commentary
THAT   E. Jenni and C. Westermann (eds.), *Theologisches
          Handwörterbuch zum Alten Testament*, 2 vols.
          (Munich: Chr Kaiser Verlag, 1971–76)
TOTC   Tyndale Old Testament Commentaries

Bible versions

GNT   The Good News Bible, The Bible in Today's English
           Version. New Testament © 1966, 1971, 1976 by the
           American Bible Society.
NIV   The Holy Bible, New International Version
           (Anglicized edition). Copyright © 1979, 1984, 2011
           by Biblica. Used by permission of Hodder &
           Stoughton Ltd, an Hachette UK company.
           All rights reserved. 'NIV' is a registered trademark
           of Biblica. UK trademark number 1448790.
NRSV   The New Revised Standard Version of the Bible,
           Anglicized Edition, copyright © 1989, 1995 by the
           Division of Christian Education of the National
           Council of the Churches of Christ in the USA.
           Used by permission. All rights reserved.
RSV   The Revised Standard Version of the Bible,
           copyright © 1946, 1952 and 1971 by the Division of
           Christian Education of the National Council of the
           Churches of Christ in the USA. Used by permission.
           All rights reserved.

SELECT BIBLIOGRAPHIES

Nahum

Baker, D. W. (1988), *Nahum, Habakkuk and Zephaniah: An Introduction and Commentary*, TOTC (Leicester: Inter-Varsity Press).

Barker, K. L. and W. Baily (1999), *Micah, Nahum, Habakkuk, Zephaniah*, New American Commentary 25 (Nashville: Broadman & Holman).

Benka, D. (2014), 'Power of the Powerless and the Powerless Power: A Reading of Nahum', *Biblische Notizen* 161: 3–18.

Boda, M. J. (2017), 'Freeing the Burden of Prophecy: *Maśśāʾ* and the Legitimacy of Prophecy in Zechariah 9 – 14', in *Exploring Zechariah*, vol. 2: *The Development and Role of Biblical Traditions in Zechariah*, Ancient Near East Monographs 17 (Atlanta: SBL), pp. 135–152.

Christensen, D. L. (1987), 'The Acrostic of Nahum Once Again: A Prosodic Analysis of Nahum 1, 1–10', *Zeitschrift für die alttestamentliche Wissenschaft* 99: 409–415.

Clark, D. J. and H. A. Hatton (1989), *A Handbook on the Books of Nahum, Habakkuk, and Zephaniah*, UBS Handbook Series (New York: United Bible Societies).

Coggins, R. J. (1985), *Israel among the Nations: A Commentary on the Books of Nahum and Obadiah*, International Theological Commentary (Grand Rapids: Eerdmans).

Coggins, R. J. and J. H. Han (2011), *Six Minor Prophets through the Centuries: Nahum, Habakkuk, Zephaniah, Haggai, Zechariah and Malachi*, Blackwell Bible Commentaries (Malden, MA: Wiley-Blackwell).

Cook, G. (2016), 'Nahum's Prophetic Name', *Tyndale Bulletin* 67: 37–40.

Dietrich, W. (2016), *Nahum, Habakkuk, Zephaniah*, IECOT (Stuttgart: Kohlhammer).

Elliger, K. (1975), *Das Buch der zwölf kleinen Propheten II: Die Propheten Nahum, Habakuk, Zephanja, Haggai, Sacharja, Maleachi*, Das Alte Testament Deutsch 25 (Göttingen: Vandenhoeck & Ruprecht).

Floyd, M. H. (2000), *Minor Prophets*, FOTL 22.2 (Grand Rapids: Eerdmans).

Goldingay, J. and P. J. Scalise (2009), *Minor Prophets II*, NIBC (Peabody, MA: Hendrickson).

Jeremias, J. (2018), 'Ein neues Gottesbild: Die programmatischse Eröffnung des Buches Nahum', *Zeitschrift für die alttestamentliche Wissenschaft* 130(2): 217–234.

Jones, B. A. (2016), 'The Seventh-Century Prophets in Twenty-First Century Research', *Currents in Biblical Research* 14: 129–175.

La Sor, W. S., D. A. Hubbard and F. W. Bush (1982), *Old Testament Survey: The Message, Form and Background of the Old Testament* (Grand Rapids: Eerdmans).

Longman, T. (1999), 'Nahum', in T. E. McComiskey (ed.), *The Minor Prophets: An Exegetical and Expository Commentary*, vol. 2: *Obadiah, Jonah, Micah, Nahum and Habakkuk* (2nd printing; Grand Rapids: Baker), pp. 765–829.

Marti, K. (1904), *Das Dodekapropheton*, KHAT 13 (Tübingen: Mohr Siebeck).

Noetzel, J. (2015), *Maleachi, ein Hermeneut*, BZAW 467 (Berlin: de Gruyter).

Nogalski, J. D. (2003), 'The Day(s) of YHWH in the Book of the Twelve', in P. L. Redditt and A. Schart (eds.), *Thematic Threads in the Book of the Twelve*, BZAW 325 (Berlin: de Gruyter), pp. 192–213.

—— (2011), *The Book of the Twelve: Micah–Malachi*, SHBC (Macon, GA: Smyth & Helwys).

Peels, H. G. L. (1993), '*Voed het oud vertrouwen weder*':
  De Godsopenbaring bij Nahum, Apeldoornse Studies 28
  (Kampen: Kok).
Renz, T. (2009), 'A Perfectly Broken Acrostic in Nahum 1',
  The Journal of Hebrew Scriptures 9, art. 23, <https://doi.org/
  10.5508/jhs.2009.v9.a23>.
Roberts, J. J. M. (1991), *Nahum, Habakkuk and Zephaniah*, Old
  Testament Library (Louisville: Westminster/John Knox).
Robertson, O. P. (1990), *The Books of Nahum, Habakkuk and
  Zephaniah*, NICOT (Grand Rapids: Eerdmans).
Rudolph, W. (1975), *Micha, Nahum, Habakuk, Zephanja*, KAT 13.3
  (Gütersloh: Gütersloher Verlagshaus).
Smith, R. L. (1984), *Micah–Malachi*, Word Biblical Commentary 32
  (Waco: Word).
Spronk, K. (1997), *Nahum*, HCOT (Kampen: Kok).
—— (1998), 'Acrostics in the Book of Nahum', *Zeitschrift für die
  alttestamentliche Wissenschaft* 110: 209–222.
—— (2018), 'The Avenging God of Nahum as Comforter of the
  Traumatised', Festschrift S. D. (Fanie) Snyman, *Acta Theologica
  Supplementum* 26: 237–250.
Sweeney, M. A. (1992), 'Concerning the Structure and Generic
  Character of the Book of Nahum', *Zeitschrift für die
  alttestamentliche Wissenschaft* 104: 364–377.
—— (2000), *The Twelve Prophets 2*, Berit Olam (Collegeville, MN:
  Liturgical).
Timmer, D. (2012), 'Nahum, Prophet of God Who Avenges
  Injustice', in H. G. L. Peels and S. D. Snyman (eds.), *The Lion
  Has Roared: Theological Themes in the Prophetic Literature of the Old
  Testament* (Eugene: Pickwick), pp. 79–86.
Tuell, S. (2016), *Reading Nahum–Malachi: A Literary and Theological
  Commentary* (Macon, GA: Smyth & Helwys).
van der Woude, A. S. (1985), *Jona–Nahum*, POT (Callenbach:
  Nijkerk).
Vermeulen, K. (2017), 'The Body of Nineveh: The Conceptual
  Image of the City in Nahum 2 – 3', *Journal of Hebrew Scriptures*
  17, <https://doi.org/10.5508/jhs.2017.v17.a1>.
Wessels, W. J. (1998), 'Nahum, an Uneasy Expression of Yahweh's
  Power', *Old Testament Essays* 11: 615–628.

Wessels, W. J. (2006), 'Nahum 2: A Call to Witness a Display of Yahweh's Power', *Journal for Semitics* 15: 544–563.

—— (2014a), 'Nahum', in G. A. Yee, H. R. Page Jr and M. J. M. Coomber (eds.), *Fortress Commentary on the Bible: The Old Testament and Apocrypha* (Minneapolis: Fortress), pp. 885–891.

—— (2014b), 'Subversion of Power: Exploring the Lion Metaphor in Nahum 2:12–14', *Old Testament Essays* 27: 703–721.

—— (2018), 'Cultural Sensitive Readings of Nahum 3:1–7', *HTS / Theological Studies* 74(1): 4931, <https://doi.org/10.4102/hts.v74i1.4931>.

Weyde, K. W. (2018), 'Once Again the Term *maśśā'* in Zechariah 9:1; 12:1 and in Malachi 1:1: What Is Its Significance?', Festschrift S. D. (Fanie) Snyman, *Acta Theologica Supplementum* 26: 251–267.

Willi-Plein, I. (2006), 'Wort, Last oder Auftrag? Zur Bedeutung von *maśśā'* in Überschriften prophetischen Texteinheiten', in R. Lux and E. J. Waschke (eds.), *Die unwiderstehliche Wahrheit: Studien zur alttestamentlichen Prophetie; Festschrift für Arndt Meinhold*, Arbeiten zur Bibel und ihrer Geschichte 26 (Leipzig: Evangelische Verlagsanstalt), pp. 431–438.

Zenger, E. (ed.) (2008), *Einleitung in das Alte Testament*, Kohlhammer Studienbücher Theologie 1.1 (Stuttgart: Kohlhammer).

Habakkuk

Achtemeier, E. (1986), *Nahum–Malachi*, Interpretation (Atlanta: John Knox).

Andersen, F. I. (2001), *Habakkuk*, Anchor Bible 25 (New York: Doubleday).

Anderson, J. E. (2011), 'Awaiting an Answered Prayer: The Development and Reinterpretation of Habakkuk 3 in Its Contexts', *Zeitschrift für die alttestamentliche Wissenschaft* 123: 57–71.

Baker, D. W. (1988), *Nahum, Habakkuk and Zephaniah: An Introduction and Commentary*, TOTC (Leicester: Inter-Varsity Press).

Barker, K. L. and W. Baily (1999), *Micah, Nahum, Habakkuk, Zephaniah*, New American Commentary 25 (Nashville: Broadman & Holman).

Boda, M. J. (2017), 'Freeing the Burden of Prophecy: *Maśśā'* and the Legitimacy of Prophecy in Zechariah 9 – 14', in *Exploring Zechariah*, vol. 2: *The Development and Role of Biblical Traditions in Zechariah*, Ancient Near East Monographs 17 (Atlanta: SBL), pp. 135–152.

Bratcher, D. R. (1984), 'The Theological Message of Habakkuk: A Literary-Rhetorical Analysis', PhD dissertation, Union Theological Seminary, Virginia.

Bruce, F. F. (1999), 'Habakkuk', in T. E. McComiskey (ed.), *The Minor Prophets: An Exegetical and Expository Commentary*, vol. 2: *Obadiah, Jonah, Micah, Nahum and Habakkuk* (2nd printing; Grand Rapids: Baker), pp. 831–896.

Clark, D. J. and H. A. Hatton (1989), *A Handbook on the Books of Nahum, Habakkuk, and Zephaniah*, UBS Handbook Series (New York: United Bible Societies).

Coggins, R. J. and J. H. Han (2011), *Six Minor Prophets through the Centuries: Nahum, Habakkuk, Zephaniah, Haggai, Zechariah and Malachi*, Blackwell Bible Commentaries (Malden, MA: Wiley-Blackwell).

Dietrich, W. (2016), *Nahum, Habakkuk, Zephaniah*, IECOT (Stuttgart: Kohlhammer).

Elliger, K. (1975), *Das Buch der zwölf kleinen Propheten II: Die Propheten Nahum, Habakuk, Zephanja, Haggai, Sacharja, Maleachi*, Das Alte Testament Deutsch 25 (Göttingen: Vandenhoeck & Ruprecht).

Floyd, M. H. (1993), 'Prophecy and Writing in Habakkuk 2, 1–5', *Zeitschrift für die alttestamentliche Wissenschaft* 105: 462–481.

—— (2000), *Minor Prophets*, FOTL 22.2 (Grand Rapids: Eerdmans).

Gunneweg, A. H. J. (1986), 'Habakuk und das Problem des leidenden tsaddiq', *Zeitschrift für die alttestamentliche Wissenschaft* 98: 400–414.

Haak, R. D. (1992), *Habakkuk*, Vetus Testamentum Supplements 44 (Leiden: Brill).

Herrmann, W. (2001), 'Das unerledigte Problem des Buches Habakkuk', *Vetus Testamentum* 51: 481–496.

Hiebert, T. (1986), *God of My Victory: The Ancient Hymn in Habakkuk 3*, Harvard Semitic Monographs 38 (Atlanta: Scholars Press).

Holladay, W. L. (2001), 'Plausible Circumstances for the Prophecy of Habakkuk', *Journal of Biblical Literature* 120: 123–130.

Janzen, J. G. (1982), 'Eschatological Symbol and Existence in Habakkuk', *Catholic Biblical Quarterly* 44: 394–414.

Johnson, M. D. (1985), 'The Paralysis of Torah in Habakkuk I 4', *Vetus Testamentum* 35: 257–266.

Keller, C. A. (1985), 'Die Eigenart der Prophetie Habakuks', *Zeitschrift für die alttestamentliche Wissenschaft* 85: 156–167.

Koehler, L. and W. Baumgartner (eds.) (1958), *Lexicon in Veteris Testamenti Libros* (Leiden: Brill).

Koenen, K. (1994), *Heil den Gerechten – Unheil den Sündern! Ein Beitrag zur Theologie der Prophetenbücher*, BZAW 229 (Berlin: de Gruyter).

Krüger, P. A. (1987), *Die boek Habakuk* (Kaapstad: NG Kerk Uitgewers).

Moseman, R. D. (2017), 'Habakkuk's Dialogue with Faithful Yahweh', *Perspectives in Religious Studies* 44: 261–274.

Nogalski, J. D. (2011), *The Book of the Twelve: Micah–Malachi*, SHBC (Macon, GA: Smyth & Helwys).

Otto, E. (1977), 'Die Stellung der Wehe-Worte in der Verkündigung des Propheten Habakuk', *Zeitschrift für die alttestamentliche Wissenschaft* 89: 73–107.

—— (1985), 'Die Theologie des Buches Habakuk', *Vetus Testamentum* 35: 274–295.

Prinsloo, G. T. M. (1989), ''n Literêr-eksegetiese analise van die boek Habakuk', PhD dissertation, University of Pretoria, Pretoria.

—— (1999), 'Reading Habakkuk as a Literary Unit', *Old Testament Essays* 12: 515–535.

Roberts, J. J. M. (1991), *Nahum, Habakkuk and Zephaniah*, Old Testament Library (Louisville: Westminster/John Knox).

Robertson, O. P. (1990), *The Books of Nahum, Habakkuk and Zephaniah*, NICOT (Grand Rapids: Eerdmans).

Rudolph, W. (1975), *Micha, Nahum, Habakuk, Zephanja*, KAT 13.3 (Gütersloh: Gütersloher Verlagshaus).

Scott, J. M. (1985), 'A New Proposal for Habakkuk II 4–5A', *Vetus Testamentum* 35: 330–340.

Smith, R. L. (1984), *Micah–Malachi*, Word Biblical Commentary 32 (Waco: Word).

Snyman, S. D. (1996), ''n Struktureel-historiese eksegese van Habakuk 1:2 – 2:4', *Acta Theologica* 16: 68–86.

—— (2003), 'Non-violent Prophet and Violent God in the Book of Habakkuk', *Old Testament Essays* 16: 422–434.

Steeger, W. P. (1983), 'A Socio-historical Examination of Habakkuk 1 – 2', PhD dissertation, The Southern Baptist Theological Seminary.

Sweeney, M. A. (1991), 'Structure, Genre and Intent in the Book of Habakkuk', *Vetus Testamentum* 41: 63–83.

—— (2000), *The Twelve Prophets 2*, Berit Olam (Collegeville, MN: Liturgical).

Szeles, M. A. (1987), *Wrath and Mercy: A Commentary on the Books of Habakkuk and Zephaniah*, International Theological Commentary (Grand Rapids: Eerdmans).

Tuell, S. (2016), *Reading Nahum–Malachi: A Literary and Theological Commentary* (Macon, GA: Smyth & Helwys).

van der Woude, A. S. (1978), *Habakuk, Zefanja*, POT (Callenbach: Nijkerk).

van Leeuwen, C. (1996), *Habakuk: Een praktische Bijbelverklaring*, Tekst & Toelichting (Kampen: Kok).

von Rad, G. (1975), *Old Testament Theology*, vol. 1 (London: SCM).

Wever, T. (1977), *Habakuk: Dertien brieven aan een profeet, verklaring van een Bijbelgedeelte* (Kampen: Kok).

Witte, M. (2009), 'Orakel und Gebete im Buch Habakuk', in M. Witte and J. F. Diehl (eds.), *Orakel und Gebete: Interdisziplinäre Studien zur Sprache der Religion in Ägypten, Vorderasien und Griechenland in hellenistischer Zeit*, Forschungen zum Alten Testament 2.38 (Tübingen: Mohr Siebeck), pp. 67–91.

Zephaniah

Baker, D. W. (1988), *Nahum, Habakkuk and Zephaniah: An Introduction and Commentary*, TOTC (Leicester: Inter-Varsity Press).

Barker, K. L. and W. Baily (1999), *Micah, Nahum, Habakkuk, Zephaniah*, New American Commentary 25 (Nashville: Broadman & Holman).

Beck, M. (2013), 'Der Tag JHWHs: Ein Schlüsselbild für das Zwölfprophetenbuch', *Bibel und Kirche* 68: 25–31.

Ben Zvi, E. (1991), *A Historical-Critical Study of the Book of Zephaniah*, BZAW 198 (Berlin: de Gruyter).

Berlin, A. (1994), *Zephaniah*, Anchor Bible 25A (New York: Doubleday).

Clark, D. A. R. (2011), 'Reversing Genesis: A Theological Reading of Creation Undone in Zephaniah', *Expository Times* 123: 166–170.

Clark, D. J. and H. A. Hatton (1989), *A Handbook on the Books of Nahum, Habakkuk and Zephaniah*, UBS Handbook Series (New York: United Bible Societies).

Coggins, R. J. and J. H. Han (2011), *Six Minor Prophets through the Centuries: Nahum, Habakkuk, Zephaniah, Haggai, Zechariah and Malachi*, Blackwell Bible Commentaries (Malden, MA: Wiley-Blackwell).

Deissler, A. (1988), *Zwölf Propheten 3: Zefanja, Haggai, Sacharja, Maleachi*, Neue Echter Bibel 21 (Würzburg: Echter Verlag).

Dietrich, W. (2016), *Nahum, Habakkuk, Zephaniah*, IECOT (Stuttgart: Kohlhammer).

Edler, R. (1984), *Das Kerugma des Propheten Zefanja*, Freiburger Theologische Studien (Freiburg: Herder).

Elliger, K. (1975), *Das Buch der zwölf kleinen Propheten II: Die Propheten Nahum, Habakuk, Zephanja, Haggai, Sacharja, Maleachi*, Das Alte Testament Deutsch 25 (Göttingen: Vandenhoeck & Ruprecht).

Floyd, M. H. (2000), *Minor Prophets*, FOTL 22.2 (Grand Rapids: Eerdmans).

House, P. R. (1988), *Zephaniah: A Prophetic Drama*, JSOTSup 69 (Sheffield: Almond).

Kapelrud, A. S. (1975), *The Message of the Prophet Zephaniah*, Morphology and Ideas (Oslo: Universitetsforlaget).

Kirkpatrick, J. D. (1993), 'Eskatologie in die boek Sefanja', DD dissertation, University of Pretoria.

Koehler, L. and W. Baumgartner (eds.) (1958), *Lexicon in Veteris Testamenti Libros* (Leiden: Brill).

Krinetski, G. (1977), *Zefanjastudien: Motiv-und Traditionskritik und Kompositions- und Redaktionskritik*, Regensburger Studien zur Theologie (Frankfurt: Peter Lang).

Motyer, J. A. (1998), 'Zephaniah', in T. E. McComiskey (ed.), *The Minor Prophets: An Exegetical and Expository Commentary*, vol. 3: *Zephaniah, Haggai, Zechariah and Malachi* (Grand Rapids: Baker), pp. 897–962.

Nel, P. J. (1989), 'Structural and Conceptual Strategy in Zephaniah, Chapter 1', *Journal of Northwest Semitic Languages* 15: 155–168.

Nogalski, J. D. (2011), *The Book of the Twelve: Micah–Malachi*, SHBC (Macon, GA: Smyth & Helwys).

Redelinghuys, C. J. (2017), 'Creation Utterly Consumed? Towards an Eco-critical Reading of Zephaniah 1:2–6', *Old Testament Essays* 30(3): 803–818.

Roberts, J. J. M. (1991), *Nahum, Habakkuk and Zephaniah*, Old Testament Library (Louisville: Westminster/John Knox).

Robertson, O. P. (1990), *The Books of Nahum, Habakkuk and Zephaniah*, NICOT (Grand Rapids: Eerdmans).

Rudolph, W. (1975), *Micha, Nahum, Habakuk, Zephanja*, KAT 13.3 (Gütersloh: Gütersloher Verlagshaus).

Seybold, K. (1985), *Satirische Prophetie: Studien zum Buch Zefanja*, Stuttgarter Bibelstudien (Stuttgart: Katholisches Bibelwerk).

Smith, R. L. (1984), *Micah–Malachi*, Word Biblical Commentary 32 (Waco: Word).

Snyman, S. D. (1997), ''n Eksegetiese ondersoek na die teologiese inhoud van Sefanja 1:7–13', *Acta Theologica* 17: 114–127.

—— (2000a), 'In Search of Tradition Material in Zephaniah 1:7–13', *Acta Theologica* 20: 111–121.

—— (2000b), 'Violence and Deceit in Zephaniah 1:9', *Old Testament Essays* 13: 89–102.

Sweeney, M. A. (1991), 'A Form-Critical Reassessment of the Book of Zephaniah', *Catholic Biblical Quarterly* 53: 388–408.

—— (2000), *The Twelve Prophets 2*, Berit Olam (Collegeville, MN: Liturgical).

Szeles, M. A. (1987), *Wrath and Mercy: A Commentary on the Books of Habakkuk and Zephaniah*, International Theological Commentary (Grand Rapids: Eerdmans).

Timmer, D. C. (2016), 'Political Models and the End of the World in Zephaniah', *Biblical Interpretation* 24: 310–331.

Tuell, S. (2016), *Reading Nahum–Malachi: A Literary and Theological Commentary* (Macon, GA: Smyth & Helwys).

Ufok Udoekpo, M. (2010), *Re-thinking the Day of YHWH and Restoration of Fortunes in the Prophet Zephaniah: An Exegetical and Theological Study of 1:14–18; 3:14–20*, An Outline of an Old Testament Dialogue 2 (Bern: Peter Lang).

van der Woude, A. S. (1978), *Habakuk, Zefanja*, POT (Nijkerk: Callenbach).

Vlaardingerbroek, J. (1993), *Sefanja*, COT (Kampen: Kok).

von Rad, G. (1959), 'The Origin of the Concept of the Day of Yahweh', *Journal of Semitic Studies* 4: 97–108.

—— (1975), *Old Testament Theology*, vol. 1 (London: SCM).

Williams, D. L. (1961), 'Zephaniah: A Re-interpretation', PhD, Duke University.

Wright, C. J. H. (2004), *Old Testament Ethics for the People of God* (Leicester: Inter-Varsity Press).

GENERAL INTRODUCTION

The prophets were known primarily for the messages they delivered. In fact, the term 'prophet' in the Greek language denotes something of a message delivered from the gods to human beings. The Hebrew word for 'prophet' most commonly used in the Old Testament suggests a person who is called (by God) to be a prophet. Being called by God meant that prophets had to proclaim the messages they received from God. It was as if the individual prophets themselves disappeared into the background while their messages were remembered. As will be explained in the commentary on the different prophetic books, this is also true of Nahum, Habakkuk and Zephaniah. It is impossible to write a biography on any of these prophets simply because we lack personal information about them.

This observation does not mean that they were not ordinary human beings. In each book the major political and military forces of their day are mentioned. In the case of Nahum, it is Nineveh, the capital of the once-mighty Assyrian Empire, that is mentioned. In the book of Habakkuk, it is the Chaldeans, or Babylonians.

In Zephaniah, the prophecies are situated within the reign of Josiah, the king of Judah (*c.*640–609 BC). The prophets were thus well informed about the major political forces at work during their ministries. To read and interpret a prophetic book against its particular historical background is vital to a good understanding of the book. Not only were the prophets well acquainted with the major political events of their time, but they were also well informed about the current internal situation in Judah. This means that the reader of a prophetic text should also be mindful of the cultural context and practices of that time. A few examples taken from the books that are discussed will prove the point. What does it mean, for instance, when Nahum declares, *I will lift your skirts over your face* (Nah. 3:5), or when Habakkuk speaks of a theophany in which *rays flashed from his hand* (Hab. 3:4)? What cultural convictions are suggested when it is said in Zephaniah 1:9 that *all who avoid stepping on the threshold* will be punished?

To gain a better understanding of a prophetic book requires reading the book in a careful way. This means being alert to nuances in the text, mindful of the literary devices used, aware of the beginning and end of units, and sensitive to the literary genres used to convey a particular message. It also means reading the text focusing on the minute detail of every verse, while keeping an eye on the overall structure and message of the book. In the case of Nahum, Habakkuk and Zephaniah we have before us literary masterpieces in which the messages were proclaimed with the use of a variety of literary genres and devices such as wordplay, chiasmi and *inclusios*.

The content of the prophetic books is thoroughly theological. In the case of Nahum, it is stated right at the beginning of the book that it should be read as an oracle and a vision revealed to Nahum. In Habakkuk it is also said that the book contains an oracle that Habakkuk received. Zephaniah starts with *The word of the LORD* and closes with a solemn *says the LORD*. The task and duty of the prophets was to provide the people of God with a theological perspective on their lives and the conditions they had to endure. They did that by making use of the age-old theological traditions recording God's gracious acts in the history of his people and handed down to the people from generation to generation. God is known as the Creator God, the One who created everything in heaven and on earth (Gen. 1:1). God is also known as the One who made promises to Abraham, Isaac and Jacob, promising them a land, posterity and his blessing (Gen. 12 – 36). God revealed himself to Moses as YHWH, the God who delivered them from the bondage of Egypt (Exod. 1 – 14). At Sinai YHWH entered into a covenant relationship with them (Exod. 19), and he sustained them in a miraculous way during their wandering in the wilderness, eventually bringing them into the Promised Land (Josh. 1 – 24). Later on the temple became the visible symbol of YHWH's presence in the midst of his people (1 Kgs 6), and to David the promise was made of an everlasting kingdom (2 Sam. 7:14). These acts of God in the history of his people formed the source of many of the prophecies the prophets had to deliver. The people were reminded of what YHWH had done in the past and as a result of his gracious acts of deliverance were called to act accordingly. The theological traditions of the past were thus appropriated and applied to the current time. This means that the prophets were critical of the current state of affairs in the land granted to them. The people, despite YHWH's acts of love and compassion, did not worship him alone. There was the constant temptation to worship other, foreign gods. The prophets were called to confront the people with this kind of religious laxity. The prophets also did not hesitate to confront kings, the priests, (false) prophets, other religious leaders, the rulers, judges and merchants, as well as ordinary people on issues of social injustice. This is what makes the prophets interesting and relevant for our day. Their prophecies were life-related, addressing the burning issues of the day.

Prophecies concerning the future were also part of their message. The future held either doom or salvation for the people. If the people continued in their sinful ways by not worshipping YHWH and him alone, and had little or no concern about injustices in society, judgment awaited them. The flipside was equally true: if the people took heed of the warnings of the prophets and repented, judgment would be averted and salvation would await them in the future. The prophets thus first provide us with a perspective of the past, recounting God's acts of deliverance; second, they were critical of their current situation and in a fearless way spoke out against all that was wrong; and, third, they opened up a vision of the future. For a period of roughly six hundred years (750–150 BC) the prophets guided the people of God. It is remarkable that there is continuity in the messages the prophets proclaimed over so many centuries, but it is also significant to note that all the prophets received their messages from the same God.

The importance of the prophets is underlined by the fact that in New Testament times, Jesus was seen as a prophet speaking the word of God. On various occasions Jesus was recognized as Elijah, Jeremiah or one of the prophets (Matt. 16:14; Mark 6:15; 8:28; Luke 9:19; John 9:17). According to Matthew 13:57 Jesus saw himself as a prophet when he declared: 'A prophet is not without honour except in his own town and in his own home' (cf. also Luke 4:24). When Jesus entered Jerusalem, he was hailed by the crowd as 'the prophet from Nazareth in Galilee' (Matt. 21:11). The miracles Jesus performed and his teachings were testimony to the fact that he was a prophet similar to the prophets typical in Old Testament times. Yet Jesus was more than a continuation of the prophets of Old Testament times. He acted as the eschatological prophet who proclaimed and started a completely new era.

Finally, the prophetic texts should be read, and commentaries are an aid in gaining a deeper and more reliable understanding of the text. The prophetic text that originated centuries ago must also be related and applied to the current day of the exegete and the local pastor serving a congregation.

NAHUM

INTRODUCTION

The book of Nahum is a rather obscure book in the collection of the Book of the Twelve. It is all about blood-thirsty revenge on the Assyrian Empire, the capital of Nineveh and the king of Assyria – at least, this is arguably the idea most people have of Nahum. In the past, Nahum has been labelled as a narrow-minded nationalistic prophet and a predecessor of later false patriotic prophets (Peels 1993: 7; Marti 1904: 305). A sermon on Nahum is seldom heard and little attention is paid to this book in monographs on the theology of the Old Testament. Spronk (1997:14) noted that there is 'an almost complete lack of references to this prophecy in the handbooks about the theology of the Old Testament'. The book is, however, part of the canon of Scripture and therefore deserves our attention.

1. Dating the book

While nothing is known about the prophet who saw the vision (cf. the comment on 1:1), dating the book is determined by two decisive dates. We know from history that Nineveh fell to the Babylonians in 612 BC. As the book of Nahum predicts the downfall of Nineveh, one may assume that the book was written before this date. There is thus little doubt that this date provides the reader with a *terminus ad quem*. In 3:8–10 the city of No-Amon (Thebes) is mentioned as a city that has been demolished (*Her infants were dashed to pieces at every street corner*, v. 10) and whose people have been taken into captivity and exile. We know that this happened in 663 BC and therefore this date serves as a *terminus a quo*. The book of Nahum can therefore be safely dated after 663 BC but before 612 BC. To try to come to a closer date than this becomes problematic. On the one hand, one may argue that Nahum uttered his prophecy close to 663 BC when Assyria was at the zenith of its power and the memory of what had happened to No-Amon was still fresh in the minds of the people of Judah. On the other hand, it may also be argued that the book should rather be dated closer to 612 BC when there were clear indications that the Assyrian dominion was on the decline, especially after the death of Ashurbanipal between 630 and 627 BC. A safe option would be to date the book about halfway between the conquering of No-Amon (Thebes) and the final downfall of Nineveh, leaving us with a date somewhere between 650 and 640 BC. A date during the reign of Josiah seems unlikely because Assyria was already weakened by that time and did not exercise harsh control over its subjects any more. To try to pinpoint the date any closer than this borders on speculation.

Assyria's rule began with the reign of Tiglath-Pileser (745–727 BC). He made sure of his undisputed rule by subjecting the Aramean peoples to the south and the kingdom of Urartu to the north, as well as securing Assyrian dominion to the west. By 738 BC most of the countries in the vicinity of Israel and Judah had been subjected to Assyrian rule and were paying tribute to Tiglath-Pileser. After the fall of Israel in 722/721 BC Judah had to pay heavy tribute to the Assyrian ruler. Tiglath-Pileser was succeeded by Sargon II (721–705 BC), Sennacherib (705–681 BC), Esarhaddon (681–669 BC) and Ashurbanipal (669–627 BC). The time of Nahum's prophecies thus coincided with the reign of Ashurbanipal. The years following the death of Tiglath-Pileser were marked by constant rebellion, especially from the Babylonians and Egypt. It was during

Ashurbanipal's rule that he had to act against Tanutamun of Egypt. He did so decisively when he marched up the River Nile as far as No-Amon (Thebes), invaded the city and effectively destroyed it in 663 BC. Nahum refers to this incident in his prophecy in 3:8. During the later years of the reign of Ashurbanipal he was faced with increased pressure and outright rebellion from the Babylonians, Egypt and various Indo-Aryan peoples. This was especially because of the threat coming from his brother in Babylon, who was appointed king of Babylon by their father. All of these skirmishes left the once-mighty Assyrian Empire weakened. After his death Ashurbanipal was succeeded by two of his sons, and it was during the reign of his second son, Sin-shar-ishkun (629–612 BC), that the Assyrian Empire collapsed under the onslaught of Nabopolassar, the founder of the Neo-Babylonian Empire, with the help of the Medes under the command of Cyaxares. The Assyrian Empire exercised its authority with brutal force and cruelty beyond imagination. Heavy tribute was demanded, public executions were a regular sight and local populations were deported to other countries. Nineveh was known as the largest ever city at that time. It was Ashurbanipal, the king of Assyria during the ministry of Nahum, who was known in particular for killing, impaling and flaying not only unfaithful rulers but their subjects as well, small and great (Timmer 2012: 80).

The Judean king during the major part of the high point of Assyrian rule was Manasseh (687–642 BC). Manasseh had no other option than to be a willing and loyal vassal of the Assyrian Empire. Neither account of his reign in the books of Kings and Chronicles is flattering: 'He did evil in the eyes of the LORD, following the detestable practices of the nations the LORD had driven out before the Israelites' (2 Kgs 21:2). Manasseh was succeeded by his son Amon, who reigned for a short period of only two years (642–640 BC) before he was in turn succeeded by Josiah (640–609 BC). A weakened Assyria provided the opportunity for Josiah to gain some independence for Judah as a nation state. Even more important were the reforms that Josiah is known for and which are recorded in 2 Kings 22:3 – 23:25 and 2 Chronicles 34:1–2, 8–28; 35:1–24. Ten years prior to the fall of Nineveh and after the discovery of a copy of 'the Book of the Law' in the temple, Josiah embarked on a major reform in which foreign cults and practices were purged from the temple, divination and magic were suppressed, holy shrines were destroyed and worship was centralized in Jerusalem.

This is worth mentioning because none of the grave sins of Manasseh are mentioned in the book of Nahum. Other prophets did not shy away from confronting the policies and practices of the kings of Israel and Judah, calling upon them to repent of their sinful ways. It is therefore strange and unusual for a prophet to focus on the evil deeds of a foreign power and to predict the inevitable downfall of that power without even hinting at the malpractices within Judah. Equally astonishing is the fact that no mention is made of the reign of Josiah, with the regaining of Judah's independence and the reforms for which the king became famous. It seems that Nahum was focused solely on the fall of Nineveh because of the injustice and oppression exercised by the Assyrian rulers. Interestingly enough, Jonah is the only other prophet with an exclusive focus on Nineveh. The contrast couldn't be greater: in Jonah's case it is, quite contrary to Nahum's focus, not the judgment upon Nineveh that forms the focus of attention, but rather Nineveh's salvation.

2. Literary issues

Scholars are agreed in their praise of the literary quality of the book. Jerome had already noted with regard to 3:1–4 that the Hebrew text is so beautiful that no translation can match it. 'As a literary craftsman Nahum has no superior and few peers among Old Testament poets' (La Sor, Hubbard and Bush 1982: 446). Han (Coggins and Han 2011: 9) refers to Nahum as 'the poet laureate' of the so-called Minor Prophets. Spronk (1997: 6) remarks that 'on at least one point all scholars who have studied the book of Nahum agree: the author was a gifted poet'. Zenger (2008: 559) noted the powerful poetic images used in the book. Wessels (2014b: 704) comments that 'the poetic nature of the Nahum text cannot go unnoticed'. In an earlier publication Wessels (1998: 622) noted 'the poetics and the effective use of rhetoric and image' that make the book of Nahum 'an amazing piece of literature'. Indeed, reading the text of the book of Nahum reveals a wealth of literary devices such as images, similes, metaphors, alliterations, parallel-isms, chiasmi and personification, contributing to the literary quality of the various prophecies. The literary quality of the book has another advantage: the book demonstrates that on a literary level, a Judean scribe is not surpassed by his Assyrian colleagues (Spronk 2018: 250).

Scholars are divided on the issue of the composition and possible development of the book. Some scholars have detected several stages of development in the book so that it could be seen as a composition that came into being over a period of time. There are other scholars who opine that the book should be seen rather as a unity that came into being over a short period of time. It is significant in this regard that in the superscription it is stated that it is the book of the vision of Nahum. The Dutch Old Testament scholar van der Woude suggested that the book should be seen as a letter written by Nahum to the people of Judah. Although the idea of the book as a letter has not received general acceptance in scholarly circles, it does add weight to the argument that the book came into being over a rather short period of time.

a. Literary genres used

An important lens through which Nahum should be read is given in its superscription. There the book is introduced as an 'oracle' or 'vision' (or *prophecy*) concerning Nineveh. A rich variety of literary genres is found in the rest of the book. It begins with a hymn in the form of an acrostic psalm (1:2–8), which is followed by a so-called word of disputation (1:9 – 2:3). The rest of the book may be seen as prophecies of doom pronounced upon the city of Nineveh and its inhabitants, including a woe oracle (3:1–7). This rich variety of literary genres, combined with gripping images and metaphors in artistic poetic language, adds to the unique literary character of the book.

b. Textual issues

The heading, which consists of two parts, has led some scholars (Zenger 2008: 560) to believe that the book is a compilation of different parts that were put together. The Hebrew text of the book seems to have been transmitted accurately. Some scholars (Gunkel) were of the opinion that the text of Nahum needed to be restored through text-critical emendations, but more and more scholars (e.g. Spronk) are convinced that this is not necessary. In most cases, according to Spronk (1997: 3), textual 'problems can be solved by a structural analysis of the text and a close examination of the extraordinary style of the poet'. The conclusion of Spronk's detailed investigation is that 'the book of Nahum should be regarded as a well-structured unity with an intricate web of cross references throughout the book, emphasizing the divine oracles' (Spronk 1997: 5).

3. An outline of the theological message of Nahum

The most fruitful way to make an assessment of the value of Nahum is to probe the theological content of the book. Otherwise the book can easily be discarded as a work fuelling nationalistic sentiment. When the book is read with its theology in mind, it becomes clear that it presents the reader with a radical focus on God. The focus on God becomes apparent when the semi-acrostic poem right at the beginning of the book is taken into consideration. This poem/psalm functions as a lens through which the rest of the book should be read. In Nahum 1:2–8 YHWH is revealed as both a jealous and an avenging God, a God slow to anger and good, a refuge in times of trouble. God is also revealed as the powerful God, whose mighty power can be witnessed in nature. Clouds are like the dust of his feet, mountains quake in his presence and hills melt away; in fact, the whole earth trembles in his presence. If this is God, and if this is a witness to his awesome power, then the only conclusion is that he is far mightier than any other worldly power, including the Assyrian Empire. This multi-faceted perspective on God confronts readers at once with their own (sometimes one-sided) views of God. God is far greater than our perception of him.

This mighty God is also the God of justice because he does not leave the guilty unpunished (1:3). God's justice extends not only to his own people but indeed to all people (an emphasis also found in the rest of the *corpus propheticum*). God is God not only of nature but of world powers as well. God's justice is then manifested in his wrath upon Nineveh. Nineveh has been found guilty of the most awful acts of injustice against other nations. It is important to note that not only Assyria's treatment of Judah is addressed here, but the injustices committed by Assyria in general against all its subjects.

Although Judah deserves to be afflicted because of God's justice (1:12), the Assyrian Empire has now overstepped the limits in dishing out punishment. God's justice demands that Assyria be reprimanded for its abuse of power. Judah may therefore expect redemption and restoration, but not as the result of its own efforts to gain independence. Judah is not called to take up arms against the Assyrian powers, with a divine promise of sure victory. In fact, Judah has no role to play in the eventual downfall of the Assyrian Empire; the victory foreseen does not belong to Judah but to YHWH. It is noteworthy that no mention is made of the king of Judah or of Jerusalem as the capital of Judah. The power to destroy Nineveh lies with YHWH alone.

The demise and eventual fall of Nineveh as the capital of the Assyrian Empire is described in graphic language. Instead of attacking other nations and seizing their territory, Assyria will now have to defend the city against an attack from an unnamed military force. However, its attempts to defend the city will be to no avail and the city will be plundered *from all its treasures* (2:9). Utter devastation and total destruction await Nineveh. God has entered into a battle with Nineveh and therefore Nineveh is humiliated in taunts likening it to a harlot whose nakedness is exposed. Its once-fearsome soldiers are described as men with melting hearts, trembling bodies and pale faces (2:10). The officials are like people who are dizzy and sleepy, stripped of the power they used to have (3:18). What is more, history proves the point Nahum wants to make. Just as the Assyrians once invaded and captured the city of No-Amon (Thebes) against all odds, so the same will happen to Assyria. What they had once done to No-Amon (Thebes) will now be done to them. When Nineveh fell, it was clear that Nahum was indeed a true prophet of God according to the criterion set by the book of Deuteronomy 18:15-22: what Nahum had said was fulfilled in the fall of Nineveh.

God acts against Assyria not only because he is the God of justice but also because his honour is at stake. Nineveh dared to plot evil against YHWH (1:9–11) and precisely because of that they will have to suffer the humiliation of total defeat. The gods revered by the Assyrians in *the temple of your gods*, together with the carved images, will be destroyed (1:14). Not only the Assyrians will stand powerless against YHWH, but the gods of Assyria will be of no help and will be equally powerless as they will also be destroyed. The view of Timmer (2012: 83) is to the point: 'YHWH will judge Assyria not because it is nationally or culturally different from Judah, but because it is the primary expression of obdurate opposition to the God of Israel in the seventh century.' At crucial points in the book the reader is reminded that although it is a foreign military force that will defeat the Assyrians, it will happen because *'I am against you,' declares the Lord Almighty* (2:13; 3:5).

God's justice, manifested in his wrath and vengeance against the Assyrian superpower, creates hope: hope for the people of Judah and hope for the individual. The people may dare to hope for a better future, free from the tyranny of Assyria, because the cruel and terrible reign of the brutal oppressor will come to an end. The proclamation of Nineveh's fall is good news and holds the promise of peace (1:15) and that festivals may once again be celebrated. The people of Judah may have hope even in the midst of the terror of Assyrian oppression because the splendour of Jacob and Israel will be restored. In the end, oppressive world powers yield to the power of God. Quite significantly, there is no mention of the sins of either Judah or the king.

The book of Nahum is a book of hope also for the individual who may be on the brink of losing hope in the midst of violence and oppression. In a recent publication, Spronk (2018: 237–250) opened up a new avenue in the appreciation of Nahum. He maintains that one obtains a different picture when reading the book of Nahum according to the hermeneutics of trauma (2018: 238) in the sense that even potentially harmful texts may have healing capacities (2018: 239). In the light of the suffering Judah had to endure because of the cruel oppression of the Assyrians, 'it is necessary to regain confidence in the knowledge that evil will be punished. Only in this way can the confidence in YHWH as the "good" God by whom one finds "shelter in days of distress"' be restored' (2018: 246). What is claimed right at the beginning of the book, that YHWH will not leave the guilty unpunished (1:3), is proved to be true. Evil, no matter how powerful, 'will be punished' (2018: 246). This deep conviction is what gives hope to believing human beings even in the midst of oppression of the worst kind. It is a hope that enables one to endure terrible hardship.

The book of Nahum thus reveals God to us in a unique way. He is at the same time the good God as well as the God who takes vengeance and is filled with wrath. His wrath is a manifestation of his righteousness. He is the mighty God of nature as well as the mighty God of world events, and therefore his people may put their trust in him and, in so doing, keep on hoping for a future of peace.

ANALYSIS

Although the book of Nahum consists of only three chapters, there is little or no consensus on the different units that make it up. The approach followed here is to focus on the larger units rather than breaking the book up into minute sub-units.

A. The superscription to the book (1:1)
B. A semi-acrostic poem-cum-psalm (1:2–8)
C. God is both judge and Saviour (1:9 – 2:2)
D. Nineveh's demise (2:3–13)
E. Prophecies announcing doom upon the Assyrian Empire, the city of Nineveh and the king of Assyria (3:1–19)

COMMENTARY

A. The superscription to the book (1:1)

Context

The heading to the book consists of two parts. The first part informs the reader that the proclamation of the message is all about Nineveh, while the second part provides the reader with knowledge about the nature of the book: it is a book about a vision revealed to a prophet by the name of Nahum who came from a place known as Elkosh. The mention of Nineveh immediately provides some context to the book. Nineveh was the capital of the Assyrian Empire which fell in 612 BC (cf. the Introduction for more information on the historical background).

Comment

1. In Hebrew, the first verse of this book consists of only six words but it contains a wealth of information that is important for understanding the rest of the book. The very first word (*maśśā'* in Hebrew, translated as *a prophecy*, or 'an oracle') is the first indication of what one may expect from the rest of the book. The noun used is also found in the other prophetic books of the Old Testament (Isa. 13:1; 14:28; 15:1; 17:1; 19:1; 21:1, 11, 13; 22:1; 23:1; 30:6; Jer. 23:33–40; Ezek. 12:10), and in Habakkuk 1:1; Zechariah 9:1; 12:1; and Malachi 1:1 it serves as a heading for an entire prophetic book, or, as in the case of Zechariah, for a new section within the book. The noun translated as *prophecy* also has the notion of 'burden' or 'load', suggesting that the oracle is a kind of burden upon the prophet that has to be delivered. The noun can also be rendered 'message', 'announcement' or 'proclamation'. Recent research on the term suggests that it can refer to a renewal of prophecy along the lines of earlier prophecy (Boda 2017: 138–152) or that written oracles or

collections of visions and words that were not heard by their audience are meant (Willi-Plein 2006: 431–438), as is indeed suggested in this verse. Another possibility is to render the term as an indication of a true prophetic oracle (Noetzel 2015: 46–47). Closely connected to the term is also the notion of divine revelation (Weyde 2018: 264). It is thus a message carrying divine authority that can be regarded as a true prophetic word. The first word is, then, a clear indication of the importance of what will be revealed in the rest of the book.

The second word in the heading refers to the capital of the Assyrian Empire, Nineveh, and would immediately have attracted the attention of the readers of this prophetic book. Nineveh was the royal capital of Sennacherib (705–681 BC), king of the Assyrian Empire, which dominated world affairs until the fall of the empire with the destruction of the city in 612 BC (cf. the Introduction for more on the historical context). It was during the reign of the Assyrians that the northern kingdom, Israel, ceased to exist as a separate state, never to regain its status as an independent country, while the southern kingdom, Judah, was firmly under its control for almost a century. Bad news for Nineveh would no doubt be good news for Judah. It is also suggested that the city of Nineveh, as the capital of the Assyrian Empire, became a symbolic name for all the forces of evil, in the same way as the city of Babylon in the book of Revelation in the New Testament.

In the second part of verse 1 the book of Nahum is further characterized as a *book of the vision*. The book of Nahum is the only one within the corpus of the prophetic literature of the Old Testament/Hebrew Bible to be called a *book* (*seper* in Hebrew) in its superscription. An interesting interpretation of the term *book* was offered by the Dutch Old Testament scholar van der Woude. According to him, *book* should be understood as a letter written from Assyria and addressed to Judah. Nahum's prophecy was then never intended to be spoken by the prophet; it was from the start meant to be put in writing as a letter (van der Woude 1985: 77–78). His proposal, interesting as it is, never found a following, and scholars are in agreement that we should think of a book rather than a letter in this case. It is significant that Nahum is put together as a book intended to be read. One should, however, be careful not to think of a 'book' as we currently think of one, containing a certain number of pages between a front and a back cover. 'Book' here probably refers to a kind of a written document that contains the vision that was 'seen' by the prophet Nahum. The content of the book came to Nahum in the form of a vision. It was thus something revealed to him, indicating divine revelation. The relationship between the initial vision seen by Nahum and the content of that vision now contained in a book is problematic. Is Nahum, the prophet to whom the vision was revealed, also the author of the book?

Nahum is the name of the person who was the recipient of the vision and as a proper noun it occurs only here in the Old Testament/Hebrew Bible. The name *Nahum* means 'comforter' (from the Hebrew *nḥm*) and it is thought to be an appropriate name for the prophet who will comfort the people with his message of the imminent downfall of Nineveh. However, too much must not be made of the connection between the name of the prophet and the message he had to deliver. Nahum is further identified as *the Elkoshite*, indicating that he came from a place called Elkosh, a geographical detail that is not found elsewhere in the Old Testament/Hebrew Bible. Consequently, it is difficult to locate the town in Judah, and suggestions that it refers to a town in the vicinity of Galilee or a place near Nineveh are nothing more than speculation. Interestingly, Spronk (1997: 32) suggested that Elkosh may not be an indication of the hometown of Nahum at all but that the word should rather be divided into two parts, *El* (God), and the Hebrew *qāšâ*, meaning '(to be) severe'. The idea then conveyed would be that a severe message from God could be expected in this book.

Meaning

Nothing else is known about the prophet: Was he married? Did he have any children? At what age was he when he received this vision? What happened to him after the vision? Was he, like Amos, a farmer, or was he considered to be a cult prophet? Perhaps there is a reason for the little information we have not only about Nahum but about all Old Testament prophets. It is not the prophet that is important, and therefore no biography of any prophet can be written. What is important is the message each prophet delivered.

Their prophetic messages are their lasting legacy, so much so that
they are still read and studied today. Three other prophets are also
identified by the towns they came from: Jeremiah, from the town
of Anathoth; Amos, from Tekoa; and Micah, from Moresheth.

B. A semi-acrostic poem-cum-psalm (1:2–8)

Context
Nahum 1:2–8 is a complex literary unit. It is presented as an acrostic
psalm following the sequence of the letters of the Hebrew alphabet,
which is impossible to replicate in a translation. However, unlike
other acrostic psalms, for instance, in the Psalter (cf. Pss 9 – 10; 111;
112; 145), the acrostic psalm presented here is incomplete as it
comes to an unexpected end at the letter 'k' (*kaph* in Hebrew),
halfway through the twenty-two letters of the Hebrew alphabet.
What complicates the matter further is that some letters of the
alphabet are skipped in the psalm. The psalm starts with the first
three letters of the Hebrew alphabet in verses 2a, 3b and 4a, but
there is no 'd' (*daleth* in Hebrew) in the next line. The line that
should have started with a 'z' (*zayin*) actually starts with 'l' (*lamed*),
and the *zayin* is only to be found in the second word of verse 6b. In
the line supposed to start with a 'j' (*yod*), the first letter is actually
a 'w' (*waw*), which is then followed by a *yod*.

   This incomplete acrostic psalm in a prophetic book raises a
number of questions. Is this psalm actually part of an already
existing psalm quoted here for the purpose of introducing Nahum's
message as a whole? There is little doubt that verses 2–8 do represent an acrostic psalm. There is also almost universal agreement
that Nahum quoted this psalm and that it was not an original composition by the prophet himself. The fact that in the entire book of
Nahum *El* is used as a name for God only here in 1:2 serves as an
argument in this regard.

   However, if it is part of an existing psalm, why quote only
the first half of the psalm? Of course, this question is based on the
assumption that because only the first half of the Hebrew alphabet
appears in the psalm, there must be a second part now lost to us.
Yet it may be that the psalm as we have it now recorded in the book
of Nahum is indeed the complete psalm.

Nahum 1:2–8 is made up of two parts: verses 2–3a consist of a statement of who God is, and verses 3b–8 are a description of a theophany in nature.

Comment

2–3a. The first part of verse 2 is structured in a skilful chiastic way: (A) God of jealousy; (B) YHWH of vengeance; (B′) YHWH of vengeance; (A′) master of wrath. The second part of verse 2 is structured as a parallelism: (A) YHWH of vengeance; (B) his foes; (A) his wrath; (B) his enemies.

Thus God is introduced and described with three terms: *jealous*, *vengeance* and *wrath*. That God is a *jealous* God is found elsewhere in the Old Testament/Hebrew Bible (Josh. 24:19; Deut. 4:24; 5:9; 6:15; Exod. 20:5). It is a characteristic of God that he demands exclusive loyalty to himself. He is not willing to allow other gods to be worshipped alongside him. In the Ten Commandments YHWH is also described as a jealous God in the context of the commandment not to worship idols. God is not willing to share his honour or power with any other god. That God is depicted as a jealous God conveys the idea of the zeal of God for his people and should therefore be understood as a covenantal term. God is jealous because of the covenant relationship between himself and his people.

The second term used to describe God is *vengeance*. This is an important designation for God as it is repeated no less than three times: YHWH is an avenger. YHWH's vengeance is best understood within the context of justice and of injustices committed. YHWH's vengeance is activated by injustices and his resolve to restore justice and righteousness. When YHWH exercises his vengeance, it is not vengeance for the sake of vengeance, but it is vengeance for the sake of bringing an end to injustices.

The third term used to describe YHWH is *wrath*. YHWH is literally 'a *ba'al* of wrath', that is, a master or lord of wrath. God can become angry. His anger also has to be understood in terms of the covenant relationship between himself and his people. Where YHWH is not worshipped as the one and only God, his anger is provoked. His anger is further provoked by the injustices committed by human beings. The vengeance of God is not directed at his people but at his *foes*, his *enemies*, presumably the Assyrians.

God is at the same time *slow to anger* (literally 'long of nose') and *great in power.* The poem draws here on an age-old confession of who God is (Exod. 34:6–7). This so-called 'grace formula' is referred to four times in the Book of the Twelve (Joel 2:13; Jon. 4:2; Mic. 7:18; Nah. 1:3). He is at once the patient God and great in power. When all these attributes of God are put together, there can be only one conclusion: guilty sinners will be punished.

Thus in the first verses of Nahum we encounter God. God is revealed not in a one-sided way, as either the God of vengeance or the God of endless patience. Rather, God is both the jealous and avenging God, and the God who is slow to anger and great in power.

3b–4. In verses 3b–8 there is a shift to a description of a theophany in the terrifying forces of nature. God is also revealed in nature; YHWH can be observed in a *whirlwind* and a *storm. Clouds* are compared to *dust* like that stirred up by people when they walk along roads. God is depicted as the mighty rider of clouds (Ps. 68:4; Isa. 14:14). The image should be understood against the background of Canaanite religion, in which Baal was the rider of clouds, making use of the forces of thunder and lightning in a storm. Verse 3b makes it clear that YHWH and not Baal is the one with the power to ride the clouds. YHWH's way can be seen and followed in the wind and the storms. The picture of YHWH revealing himself in whirlwind, storm and clouds recalls the events at Mount Sinai, when he came down to the mountain in cloud and wind. The mighty God making use of the forces of nature is at the same time the God of the covenant at Mount Sinai.

Great masses of water especially in normally dry parts of land can be destructive. The flooding of rivers can cause havoc, and the sea has something ominous to it. In Canaanite religion, Baal had to defeat Yam, the god of the sea and rivers, and in doing so he became the chief god in the Canaanite pantheon. God does more than defeat the sea and the mighty rivers: he causes them to dry up. The drying up of the sea recalls what once happened at the Red Sea, where the sea dried up and Israel was finally delivered from the bondage of Egypt (Exod. 14:15–31; 15:8; cf. Pss 66:6; 106:9; Hab. 3:8–15). The message is clear: in the present, God is in control of nature, and just as in the past when YHWH once delivered his people by parting the sea, so it will happen again when Assyria is defeated. *Bashan*, *Carmel* and *Lebanon* (Isa. 33:9), all situated in the northern part of Israel, were places known for their fertility. These places will *fade* and *wither*, most probably because of a severe drought. Both the land covered by water (sea and river) and the fertile land are under God's control. Creation in its totality will be affected by the theophany about to happen.

5. Verse 5 describes the reaction of nature to the awesome appearance of YHWH. *Mountains quake* and *hills* are about to (metaphorically speaking) *melt away*. Even the mountains and hills that are regarded as symbols of everlasting stability will shake and melt. The shaking, moving and melting of mountains and hills are also associated with an earthquake that will accompany the theophany of YHWH, as is often the case elsewhere in the Old Testament (Judg. 5:4; Pss 46:3; 68:8; Isa. 13:13; Jer. 4:24; Ezek. 38:19–20; Joel 3:16; Amos 9:5; Hab. 3:6). Human beings will also be affected. The universal consequences of the theophany described are noteworthy. Not only the sea and the rivers, but also the land (*mountains*, *hills*, *earth* and *world*) and finally also people will witness and experience the coming of YHWH.

6. The description of the theophany leads to a rhetorical question in verse 6: who will be able to face and *withstand* the coming of YHWH (Jer. 10:10; Amos 7:2; Mal. 3:2)? YHWH's indignation, his fierce anger and wrath, will be unbearable. The image of *fire* being *poured out* conveys the sense of total destruction just as a fire consumes everything in its path. Likewise, even hard *rocks* will be crumbled into pieces. Just as it is impossible to put crumbled pieces of rock back together again, so the destruction of the enemy will be total, with no possibility of restoration. Therefore, the answer to the question is simple: no-one will be able to endure the coming judgment of YHWH. In the light of the effects YHWH's coming will have on nature, it is unthinkable that human beings might be able to resist the impact. Although Assyria is not mentioned by name, it is assumed that if nobody will be able to endure the wrath of YHWH, Assyria will certainly not be able to do so either.

7–8. YHWH is the God who is revealed as jealous and avenging, coming in a mighty theophany to judge and punish the guilty. Yet he is slow to anger (cf. v. 3), and in verse 7 it is also said that he is *good*, and that he is a stronghold or shelter in the day of distress. Confession of God as good is found often in the Psalms (25:8; 34:8; 100:5; 106:1; 107:1; 118:1; 135:3; 136:1; 145:9). The second half of verse 7 states that YHWH knows (*cares for*) those who seek shelter in him. The Hebrew word (*yd'*, 'to know') conveys a personal relationship of love. 'To know' is also a covenant term reminding the people that the relationship between YHWH and his people is a covenantal one, in which loyalty and mutual love are key ingredients.

With verse 8 the acrostic psalm comes to an end with the letter 'k' (*kaph* in Hebrew). While YHWH's people confess and experience him to be good, his enemies will experience the exact opposite: their place will come to an end through a *flood*. The image of water returns. In verse 4 it was said that rivers will dry up, but here in verse 8 a devastating flood will bring an end to YHWH's enemies. *Darkness* has a negative meaning – it signifies distress, dread and death. Perhaps the ninth plague of darkness (Exod. 10:21–22) is also alluded to in this verse.

Meaning

God is more than our perception of him. The way in which God is revealed in this first part of Nahum is not one-sided. God is an avenging God, but at the same time he is a God who is slow to anger. God's revelation in nature leaves one in awe, yet at the same time he is the good God and a shelter in the day of distress. The God of nature is also the covenant God who entered into a relationship with his people. The Creator God is at the same time also the God of history. The earth trembles in his presence, but so does the world and all who live in it (1:5). The book is a challenge to our perceptions of God that are also all too often one-sided. This first passage in the book serves as the foundation of what follows in the rest of the book. This is the God who will bring an end to the great capital of the Assyrian Empire and will restore the splendour of his people Israel (2:2).

C. God is both judge and Saviour (1:9 – 2:2)

Context

This section describes the total destruction awaiting Nineveh as the capital of the Assyrian Empire, while the restoration of Judah is also hinted at. Prophecies of the destruction of Nineveh (1:9–11, 14; 2:1 [2:2 in Hebrew]) alternate with prophecies of salvation for Judah (1:12–13, 15 [2:1 in Hebrew]; 2:2 [2:3]). Just like the preceding acrostic psalm where no one-sided view of YHWH is presented, here YHWH is both the one who will destroy Nineveh and the one who will restore Judah. The verses can thus be seen as an application of what has been revealed about YHWH in the acrostic psalm.

Verse 12 marks the beginning of a new section in the unit. For the first and only time in the book the well-known prophetic messenger formula – 'thus says the Lord' – occurs. Verse 13 is structured in a chiastic way: (A) I will break (B) his yoke; (B′) the bonds (A′) I will snap. The change from second-person feminine singular suffixes in verse 13 to second-person masculine singular forms in verse 14 marks an abrupt shift in attention from salvation for Judah to the eventual fall of Assyria. Verse 15 indicates another turning point in the passage by the prominent 'Look' beginning the unit. The last unit consists of 2:1–2.

Comment

9–11. No matter what the enemies of YHWH may think to plan against him, YHWH himself will bring it to an end. It is therefore futile even to *plot against* YHWH. The completeness of the destruction awaiting Nineveh is emphasized by the second part of verse 9, which says that there will be no second chance for the oppressor to cause trouble for the people of God. Verse 10 is generally seen as a difficult verse, but the general meaning is clear. In three similes the total destruction of the enemy is once again foreseen. Like *entangled thorns* vulnerable to fire, drunken people (who will have to drink from the cup of God's wrath and experience the shame of defeat) and *dry stubble* known for its inflammability, they will be consumed, presumably by fire (Exod. 15:7; Isa. 5:24; Obad. 18; Zech. 12:6; Mal. 4:1–3). Once again, a picture of total and utter destruction is painted. The same verb used in verse 9 (to think, devise, plan, plot) is used again in verse 11, thereby creating an *inclusio*. From Nineveh and, consequently, the Assyrian people, someone has *come forth* to plan *evil* against YHWH himself. This person can be none other than the king of the Assyrians. He is further characterized as the one who counsels (*devises*) *wicked plans*.

The term *wicked plans* may also be interpreted as a proper name, Belial, considered to be a demon or god. There is more at stake than a nation under threat from the Assyrians; this mighty empire even plotted against YHWH, taking advice from Belial. Yet over against the plot planned against YHWH stands YHWH's awesome power demonstrated in the theophany. Over against the evil of a foreign king and the idol he consults stands the justice of YHWH. No foreign king, nor the gods associated with him, is a match for the overwhelming power of YHWH.

12–14. The prophet proclaims a message of salvation to the people. On the one hand, the mighty Assyrian Empire will simply be cut off and will *pass away*, despite its obvious military strength and the numeric advantage of its army. The metaphor used indicates that the Assyrians will be cut off like the wool from sheep. On the other hand, Judah's affliction will soon be something of the past. Judah has had to suffer affliction not primarily because of Assyrian oppression, but because YHWH brought this affliction upon them in and through the Assyrians. This, however, will now come to an end and Judah is promised that it will never again have to suffer at the hands of the Assyrians. Verse 13 commences with *Now*, indicating that relief from suffering is at hand and will come any moment now. To emphasize this message the prophet makes use of well-known metaphors for oppression found elsewhere in the Old Testament/Hebrew Bible (Isa. 9:4; 10:27; 14:25; Ezek. 34:27). A *yoke* is used to tame an ox and put the animal under the control of the farmer. Likewise, the *shackles* referred to are used to strap the yoke onto the neck of the ox. The yoke and the shackles strapped to them, then, refer to the dominion of the Assyrians. As an ox is at the mercy of the farmer once the yoke is strapped to its neck, so Judah is under the control of the Assyrians. When the yoke is broken and the shackles are ripped off, the ox is free from the control of the farmer. Likewise, Judah will experience freedom when the Assyrian rule comes to an end soon. Spronk (1997: 73) offers an interesting alternative interpretation. According to him, *yoke* can also be interpreted as 'rod', referring to Isaiah 10:5. YHWH, then, will break the Assyrian rod, and as a result Judah will be liberated from the oppression it has suffered for so long. As is often the case in the Old Testament, one has to allow for ambiguity in the text, so that perhaps both a yoke and a rod are alluded to. Once again, as so many times elsewhere in the Bible, God's grace and love overrule his wrath, caused by the sins of his people.

The judgment pronounced upon the Assyrians is not the opinion of the prophet or the wishful thinking of anybody else in Judean society. According to verse 14, what will follow is a *command* from YHWH himself. Three terrible judgments are pronounced upon the king of Assyria. First, described with the aid of an interesting metaphor of seed being sown, there will be *no descendants* for the king. To have no descendants means that the great name he has made during his rule will come to an end, with nobody to carry it further. Even today, politicians wish to leave a lasting legacy so that their names will be remembered and honoured by future generations. Here, however, a famous and seemingly invincible dynasty will come to a complete end. Second, the gods worshipped by the king will be destroyed by being taken out of the temples. Kings relied on the support of the gods to succeed in their military campaigns. The gods, in turn, could then rely on the worship of the king. Third, YHWH will dig a *grave* for the king, where he will be buried. According to Roberts (1991: 54), this means that there will be no family member left to bury the dead body of the king, nor will anybody else bother him- or herself with the business of burying a despised king. Then, quite significantly, a reason is given: the king is worthless (*vile*), having no significance at all. The Hebrew word used denotes the idea of being light or of little value, hence the apt translation 'worthless' by the NRSV.

15. In verse 15 something new is about to be announced. A messenger can be seen on the mountains and he is about to bring some news. The background to the announcement of a messenger approaching the city from the mountaintops (perhaps the mountains surrounding Jerusalem; cf. Ps. 125:2) is that of a messenger coming from a battleground to the city, where the citizens are waiting to hear what news he has, be it good or bad. In this case the messenger brings good news: he is a herald of *peace*. The bringing of a message of peace means that the tone of the prophecy changes from judgment to salvation. The Hebrew concept of *peace* is rich in meaning far beyond a mere cessation of hostilities

between nations; it has the meaning of wholeness or completeness,
health and vitality, as the result of justice. When the Assyrians are
defeated, justice will be restored and peace will be the result.

The words of the first half of the verse are also found in Isaiah
52:7:

> How beautiful on the mountains
>   are the feet of those who bring good news

with the small variation that the Isaiah text mentions the 'beautiful'
feet of the messenger. Opinions differ as to who said these words
first. Some scholars (Longman 1999: 799–800; Nogalski 2011: 617)
argue that it is the book of Nahum that quotes from Isaiah, while
others (Spronk 1997: 61; Sweeney 2000: 435; Goldingay and Scalise
2009: 30; Tuell 2016: 32) are convinced that it is the other way
around. Coggins (1985: 33) considers the possibility of a 'stock of
oracular material which might be used as appropriate in the particular circumstances of each collection'. Given the assumption
that Nahum is a pre-exilic book that originated during the final
days of the Assyrian rule, and that Isaiah 52 can safely be considered
as a post-exilic text, it is more likely that the Isaiah text alluded to
the Nahum text, rather than the other way around.

It is also interesting that Paul quotes this text in Romans 10:15,
though it is clear that the quote there comes from Isaiah 52:7 and
not from Nahum 1:15. The thrust of Paul's quotation of Isaiah 52:7
is that the message of the gospel of Jesus Christ must be proclaimed, and the one who proclaims this message of salvation is
like the messenger in Isaiah 52 (and, for that matter, Nah. 1:15) who
brings good news. When the good news of the gospel is accepted
and appropriated, inner peace is the result.

Once peace has been established, Judah will again have the
opportunity to *Celebrate [their] festivals*, celebrating not only the new
dawn of peace but especially the people's relationship with the God
of the covenant. It is once again God who remains true to his covenant with his people and is liberating them from the oppression
of the Assyrian Empire. This is why they are now summoned to
Celebrate [their] festivals and *fulfil [their] vows*. Exactly which festivals
the prophet has in mind is not specified, but one may think of the

main festivals like Passover, Pentecost and the festival of Booths. It is not clear what is meant by the *vows* that must be fulfilled. It seems best to understand this statement as a commitment to celebrate the festivals according to the prescriptions found in the Torah of Moses. The terrible time of Assyrian tyranny will be something of the past, never to return again.

2:1–2. The focus shifts back to the city of Nineveh. A scatterer or 'shatterer' (NRSV) has come against Nineveh. Who can be identified as the one who would scatter the Assyrians? With the benefit of hindsight, we know that it was the Medes and the Babylonians who ultimately defeated the Assyrians. It is also possible that, in a veiled way, YHWH is intended, as the one who will make use of another foreign power to liberate his people. In four brief imperatives advice is given to Nineveh: the city's inhabitants are advised to *guard the fortress* of the city, be on the lookout for an advancing army, 'gird [their] loins' (NRSV) and muster all their *strength*. Instead of attacking other nations, the Assyrians will find themselves in a position where they will be attacked and will consequently have to defend themselves against a rival.

With verse 2 the unit that began at 1:9 concludes. The verse interrupts the flow of thought between verse 1, announcing the coming of the scatterer, and verse 3, which describes the army that will come and attack the Assyrians. Once again there is a switch from judgment on Assyria to salvation for God's people. The mention of *Jacob* and *Israel* is a matter of dispute among scholars. The most plausible interpretation within the context of the unit and of the book as a whole is to interpret *Jacob* and *Israel* as honorific titles of Judah (Longman 1999: 802; Dietrich 2016: 61–62). Jacob was Israel's ancestor (Gen. 32:28; 35:10) as well as Judah's father (Gen. 29:35). Though the people have been devastated and effectively ruined, YHWH will restore them once again.

Meaning
These verses may be seen as an application of the theophany of God described in the first unit. YHWH will judge the Assyrians, but he will at the same also rescue his people.

To describe the king of the mighty Assyrian Empire as a lightweight is a provocative statement. To suggest that his dynasty will

come to an end, that the gods he worshipped will be destroyed and
that he himself will be buried in a most undignified manner is
blunt speaking! For the people of God, however, this is a message
of hope. The Assyrian oppression will not endure for ever; in fact,
the end to this reign is imminent. It is significant that although the
Assyrian king is clearly meant, he is not named. This gives this
prophecy a timeless perspective. In the course of history there have
been many tyrants and most brutal oppressors, but in the end they
perished, often in undignified ways, just like the king of Assyria
during the time of Nahum.

D. Nineveh's demise (2:3–13)

Context
In poetic language the prophet paints a vivid portrait of the imminent fall of the mighty Assyrian Empire. The focus is on the
attacking army, with the Assyrian forces defending their strongholds. This in itself will be a dramatic reversal of what the situation
used to be. The Assyrians are no longer the attacking force; they
are now in a position where they have to defend their city. The unit
can be divided into two main parts: verses 3–10 are a description
of how an army will threaten the Assyrian forces up to the point
where they will be exiled; and in verses 11–13, the metaphor of a
lion is applied to the Assyrian royal house, with the message that
eventually the hunter will become the hunted.

Comment
3–4. Although it is not explicitly stated, one may assume that
what is said in the rest of this chapter is a description of a vision
Nahum saw (cf. Nah. 1:1). Verse 3 describes the oncoming army in
a vivid way. While the purpose of describing the army was to instil
fear in the Assyrian army, for the people of God this army would
be instrumental in their eventual liberation. The soldiers described
as brave or heroes and men of power are clothed in a kind of a
crimson or scarlet uniform and carry a red-coloured shield in one
hand and a spear in the other, riding chariots ready to invade the
city. As the army is still in the process of advancing on the city,
the red on the shields does not indicate bloodstains but is simply

the colour of the shields. The overall image one gets is that of a well-organized army advancing on the city with great efficiency and ready for battle. The attacking army is not mentioned by name but, with the benefit of hindsight, we know that the Babylonians are most probably meant as, according to Ezekiel 23:14, they were known to wear red clothing in battle. Verse 4 continues the vivid description of the advance of the chariots. For those on the receiving end of this attack by a foreign military force, it might seem as if they storm like madmen through the streets, but it is all part of a well-organized army aimed at the overthrow of Assyrian dominion.

5–6. It is uncertain who is meant in verse 5: is it the attacking commander summoning his troops who speaks, or is it perhaps the king of Assyria giving orders to the soldiers under his command? The best option seems to be to interpret the text as the commander of the attacking army speaking. The second line of the verse speaks of the soldiers who *stumble on their way*, suggesting that they are advancing on the city wall rather than defending it. The troops are summoned and, apparently, stumble in their haste to make progress towards the city walls. The objective is to enter the city by breaching the city wall, while making use of a kind of screen that protects the attacking soldiers from those who defend the city. It is uncertain what is meant by the *river gates* that are *thrown open* in verse 6. Reading the text literally, it may mean that the city will be engulfed by the flooding waters of a river, perhaps the Tigris. It is, however, difficult to understand who will open the river gates, and it is also difficult to imagine how a palace built on high ground will collapse due to a flood. Reading the text metaphorically, the river flooding the city may refer to the onslaught of the advancing army such that the palace of the king will be taken, likened to the melting away of a mud structure swept away by floodwaters.

7. This verse presents the exegete with a real *crux interpretum*. The different translations offered especially for the first part of the verse provide ample proof of the difficulties one encounters in this verse. It has been *decreed* that an unnamed female be stripped or uncovered and carried away. The verb 'to uncover' may also indicate to be taken into exile (NIV *be exiled*). It is quite possible that both meanings of the word are alluded to. The identity of the

unnamed female remains a mystery. It may refer to the city of Nineveh or to the queen of Assyria, or even to the female inhabitants of the city. The fate of Nineveh is sealed as it has already been established (*decreed*). The king and his army will not be able to withstand the onslaught of an invading enemy taking the city with brutal force. Either the queen or the female inhabitants of the city, or both, will suffer the humiliation of being taken captive and carried away in exile. The female servants taken with her/them will lament and beat their 'hearts' (in the Hebrew language) in anguish because of what is happening to them as they share in the humiliation.

8–9. For the first time since the superscription to the book, *Nineveh* is now mentioned explicitly by name. Dietrich (2016: 66) noted that Nineveh is mentioned 'almost exactly in the geographical middle of the book', with twenty-three verses preceding and twenty-four verses following verse 8. The city is compared to a *pool* whose water is leaking away to eventually leave it dry. Nineveh was located close to the Tigris River and was known for its channels. It is interesting to note that the name of the city literally means 'house of fishes' (Spronk 1997: 100), suggesting an abundance of water and fish. The water metaphor was previously used in verse 6, but there the image of water served as a symbol of the invading army flooding the city; here the water draining away refers to the inhabitants and soldiers of Nineveh fleeing the city. Just as it is impossible to hold back flowing water, so it will be impossible to keep the people (citizens as well as soldiers) from fleeing the enemy in the city. Even when they are ordered to stand firm it will be to no avail. And once the people of Nineveh have left the city, it will be easy to plunder it, as verse 9 predicts will happen.

It was a generally accepted practice for an invading army to claim their victory by seizing the wealth acquired in the city or country they had conquered. Over a period of two centuries, from the time of Ashurbanipal II (884–824 BC) to Sennacherib (705–681 BC), the Assyrian kings acquired a huge volume of treasure taken from other nations. Another source to add to their wealth was the annual tribute subjected nations had to pay to the Assyrian authorities. Precious metals beyond measure in the form of gold, silver, copper and iron; military equipment such as chariots; golden objects like bowls and goblets; precious stones, furniture, garments, animals both tame and wild – all these were among the riches gathered by the Assyrians (Robertson 1990: 93). This would all change now in a dramatic way. Instead of the Assyrians plundering other nations, they themselves will now be plundered, and the silver and gold they have seized will be taken by the invading army that will defeat them. Treasures stored in the palace and temples will be looted by the victorious army.

10. Once again, the coming destruction of the city is described, this time with three staccato-like verbs making use of alliteration and assonance in an artful way. Each successive word is slightly longer than the previous one, 'making the passage sound like muffled, rolling thunder' (Dietrich 2016: 67). The physical reaction to this coming devastation is then described: *hearts* will *melt, knees give way, bodies tremble* and *faces* change colour. The once all-powerful Assyrians who ruled the known world with a brutality previously unheard of are now depicted as a people who have lost courage and strength, a fearful people who are scared to death at the prospect of what will happen to them. Although it is not said explicitly, the underlying message is that the humiliation and devastation facing Assyria are YHWH's action against them, making use of the Medes and Babylonians to accomplish this goal.

11–13. With verse 11 the metaphor of a male *lion* with *lioness, young lions* and lion *cubs* is introduced to indicate the Assyrian royal family. The male lion refers to the king of Assyria, the lioness to the queen, and the young lions and cubs refer to the princes and princesses and probably staff or state officials serving at the palace of the king. Lion imagery played an important part in Assyrian culture. Kings in the Ancient Near East, and in Assyrian art in particular, were often compared to lions, thereby indicating power, undisputed kingship and brutality. The image of a lion became a symbol of kingship. There are also Assyrian reliefs that show the king on a chariot, hunting lions (Nogalski 2011: 626; Dietrich 2016: 68). Once again, the purpose is clear: the king is seen as extremely brave and capable of taking on one of the most feared beasts of nature. The king himself is therefore even more powerful than a lion.

The unit starts off with a rhetorical question suggesting that the lions' den is nowhere to be found because it does not exist any

more. The lions' den is an obvious metaphor for the king's palace
or even the city at large. The Hebrew term used may be interpreted
as the 'pasture' of young lions, but that would seem odd as lions are
carnivores, so it seems better to understand the term as referring
to the hunting area of the lions (NIV *the place where they fed their young*).
Male lions mark as their territory an area of several square miles,
spraying their urine on plants and grass. Other male lions smell this
and do not dare to enter that area. The point the rhetorical question
wishes to make is clear: the palace and/or the city of the king and
the rest of the royal family does not exist any more because it has
all been demolished by an invading foreign military force. The king
is therefore unable to provide for his family with the treasures
robbed from subjected nations as had been done in the glorious
past.

The metaphor does not tally with what we know today about
lions and their behaviour. Lions do not have a 'den' where no-one
can disturb them. They simply roam around their marked territory
of several square miles in search of prey. Once an animal has been
caught, lions will stay in the vicinity of the carcass till it has been
devoured, and then they will move on in search of prey again. A
male lion therefore does not *fill his lairs* with torn flesh, neither does
he kill *prey for his mate*, the lioness. In fact, most of the hunting is
done by the lioness. Male lions will only take part in a hunt where
larger animals such as giraffes, buffalo or kudu are hunted. Lion
cubs will also only feed on a carcass after the male lion and the
lioness have eaten their share of the *strangled* animal. Lions do not
have natural enemies so there is no need for them to have 'moments
of calm and safety to relax, oblivious to dangers', as is sometimes
suggested (Robertson 1990: 96).

Thus, in making use of the metaphor of lions, the poem does
not apply the characteristic behaviour of lions to the king and the
royal palace, but rather the opposite: what the king does or ought
to do is transferred to what lions do. In the metaphor the male lion
does what the king does or ought to do. It is an apt metaphor
because lions are feared by most other animals, like the king who
is feared by most of his subjects.

The lion metaphor is continued in the last verse of the chapter.
In the previous two verses the male lion was described as the one

hunting to feed the young lions and the lioness. In verse 13 the hunter becomes the hunted as a *sword will devour your young lions* and there will be nothing left for the lions to prey on. As swords were not usually used to kill lions, it seems that the metaphoric language and reality are somewhat blurred. In verses 11–12 it was the young lions that were fed with prey killed by the adult lion; now the young lions are the ones who will be devoured by the sword. The effect of this killing off of young lions is clear: there is no future for the Assyrian royal kingdom. As the young lions will be killed by the sword, there will be no posterity, and consequently the royal house will simply cease to exist. Furthermore, in stark contrast to the abundance of food described in verses 11–12, there will now be nothing to eat as *no prey* will be left for them. The other nations that were subjected and raided to add to the wealth of the Assyrian Empire will not be available to them any more. The verse also drops the metaphoric language and speaks directly to what will happen to the Assyrians. YHWH will burn their *chariots* so completely that only the *smoke* of the burnt chariots will be a grim witness to the total destruction. The smoke of the burning chariots may also be a signal to others that the Assyrian warriors have been defeated (Spronk 1997: 108).

The exact meaning of the last part of the verse is difficult to determine. What is meant by the *voices of your messengers* that *will no longer be heard*? *Messengers* probably refers to those sent out to claim and reinforce the dominance of the Assyrian Empire in the entire region. This is the role of the messenger described in 1:15, who is the one who brings good news and proclaims peace. It may also be that the term refers to the messengers bringing news from the battlefield to the city, normally to proclaim yet another victory. The defeat of the army will be so devastating that no messengers will be left to bring news to the city. This pronouncement is in stark contrast to that of the herald of 1:15.

The last verse makes it clear that the real threat Nineveh and the royal house face is not a foreign invading army, but it is YHWH himself. It is *the Lord Almighty* who declares: *I am against you* (see also 3:5). It is important to note that for the first time YHWH himself speaks, bringing this unit to a climax in the form of an oracle of judgment. Similar judgment oracles, where YHWH announces

doom and destruction on foreign nations, are found elsewhere
in the Old Testament; for example, in Jeremiah 50:31; 51:25 (on
Babylon); Ezekiel 29:3; 30:22 (Egypt); 35:3 (Edom); 26:3 (Tyre);
28:22 (Sidon); and 38:3; 39:1 (Gog from Magog) (Spronk 1997: 107;
Dietrich 2016: 69). That YHWH speaks as *the LORD Almighty* is also
indicative of the fact that he will enter into a battle with Assyria.
YHWH is the Lord of the heavenly hosts who will come down to
engage in war with the opponents of YHWH.

Meaning
For many people living in well-established and stable democracies,
a situation of severe oppression by a foreign ruler is hard to
imagine. Yet, unfortunately, the harsh reality is that many people
around the globe continue to suffer from oppression, dictatorships,
a denial of basic human rights and a loss of human dignity.
Hopelessness, people simply giving up hope of a better life, is
sometimes the result. Nahum provides hope for such people. In
a situation where the enemy seems invincible, Nahum's message
is about the imminent fall of the empire! All too often, where
oppressed people are seemingly helpless, their only refuge is God.
Judah was in no position to take on the mighty Assyrian army. In
fact, nowhere in this unit is it even hinted that Judah will act in a
military way against Assyria. Judah was in no way a military threat
to Assyria, yet it has had to suffer the brutality of the Assyrians.
Nahum points the people of God to God, who will bring freedom
again just as he has done in the past. Just as God once liberated his
people from the hardships of Egypt when they were in a similarly
hopeless situation, so he will bring deliverance to his people again.

E. Prophecies announcing doom upon the Assyrian Empire, the city of Nineveh and the king of Assyria (3:1–19)

Context
Scholars have observed similarities between chapters 2 and 3. Both
the previous unit and chapter 3 commence with a description of an
attacking army. In both cases this is followed by a metaphor which
is in turn followed by a declaration by YHWH himself: 'I am against
you' (2:13; 3:5). The theme of both chapters is the imminent

destruction of the capital of the Assyrian Empire. Chapter 3, however, intensifies the picture of the downfall of Nineveh in several ways that will be pointed out in the commentary. What is particularly striking in this chapter is the short, abrupt sentences used; sometimes not even full sentences are used in the Hebrew language (Clark and Hatton 1989: 41). Scholars in general have a high regard for the quality of the poetry in this chapter. Jerome, for instance, remarked of the first four verses that no translation could do justice to the beauty of the language (Spronk 1997: 6).

Although this last chapter forms a unit, it can nevertheless be divided into the following subsections:

3:1–4: A woe oracle
3:5–7: YHWH speaks out against Assyria
3:8–10: Thebes fell and so will Nineveh
3:11–14: Nineveh is weakened and ready to be conquered
3:15–17: Nineveh will be devoured
3:18–19: Celebrate because Nineveh is mortally wounded

Comment

1–4. The very first word, *Woe*, marks this unit not only as the start of a fresh section but also as a so-called woe oracle. The cry of woe is associated with a funeral procession where mourners cry out to show their grief for the departed person. This woe cry was taken up in prophetic literature (Isa. 5:18–19; Amos 5:18–20; 6:1–7; Mic. 2:1–4; Hab. 2:6–20; Zeph. 3:1–5) to proclaim a judgment oracle indicating the certain death of those to whom the prophecy was directed. In prophetic literature, the woe oracle is used for those still living! When Nahum makes use of this term, then, it is in effect to announce the death of the capital of the Assyrian Empire. Of course, coming from Nahum, this is not a call to lament but more a reason for joy and celebration over the coming 'death' of Nineveh.

Four brief descriptions of the city are given. The Assyrians were known for their cruelty when they besieged other nations (*city of blood*). Bodies were mutilated in the most violent way and people were executed on a massive scale. The city is then also described as a city of deceit (*full of lies*). Nineveh cannot be trusted to keep the

promises it has made or the words it has uttered. The incident
recorded in 2 Kings 18:31–32 serves as a case in point. Already in
the previous chapter mention was made of the way in which Assyria
plundered the vassal states under its control to acquire wealth
beyond imagination (2:9), and here it is mentioned again (*full of
plunder*). Thinking of the different kings of the Assyrian Empire
(Tiglath-Pileser III, Sargon II, Sennacherib, Esarhaddon, Ashurbanipal) will bring back memories of how other countries have
been plundered and looted not only of material goods but of people
as well. The people captured are described as *victims* but the same
word is found in the last verse of chapter 2, where the nations
subjected to the Assyrians are described as 'prey'.

  In vivid, cryptic poetic language the battle against Assyria is
then described. It starts with a description of the attacking army
(*chariots*) followed by the weapons used (*swords* and *spears*) and finally
the effect of the attack (*piles of dead, bodies without number*). The
description of storming chariots reminds one of 2:3–4 where the
chariots were also described. There will be so many corpses that
the attacking soldiers will be *stumbling* upon them in their advance
to complete victory. The noise of the coming chariots together
with the *charging cavalry* will be followed by the silence of death as
many dead bodies will be seen on the battlefield. Interestingly
enough, no mention is made of casualties on the side of the
attacking army. A picture of a convincing victory by the attackers
and total destruction of the Assyrians is painted.

  Verse 4 differs from the previous verses. While verses 1–3 gave
a graphic description of the city of Nineveh invaded by a highly
effective attacking army, with terrible consequences, verse 4 makes
use of two metaphors to describe the city. Cities in the Ancient
Near East were often pictured as women. Here the city is likened
to two types of wicked women: a prostitute and a sorceress. Spronk
(1997: 122–123) is correct when he states that these two metaphors
represent two different kinds of evil power. Harlotry makes one
think of seduction, and sorcery includes the idea of forcing one's
will upon another. In ways not immediately clear to the present
reader of the text, Nineveh seduced nations like a prostitute
seducing men, but the price the nations eventually paid cost them
dearly in terms of tribute to the Assyrian Empire. Likewise, nations

were brought under the spell of Nineveh the sorceress, with the end result that the city now has total power to exercise its will upon other people. The scope of Nineveh's misconduct covers more than the oppression of Judah; *nations* in general are mentioned as the victims of the city. It is also possible that Ishtar, the goddess of Nineveh, is alluded to. She was revered as the goddess of love and she lured many into the power of the Assyrian Empire. Ishtar was seen as the embodiment of wifely virtues, but she also represented dangerous passions like prostitution and warfare (Tuell 2016: 42). In other parts of the Old Testament (Isa. 1:21–26; Ezek. 16; Hos. 1 – 3) the metaphor of a harlot is applied to the relationship between YHWH and Judah/Israel. Judah, as the people of God, is portrayed as a harlot but then as an unfaithful wife who has betrayed her husband (YHWH) by getting sexually involved with other men. In the New Testament, the city of Babylon is depicted as the ultimate harlot that will be destroyed (Rev. 18:9–13).

5–7. In verses 5–7 the metaphor of Nineveh as a wicked woman is continued. For the second time (cf. 2:13) YHWH speaks out against Nineveh: *'I am against you,' declares the LORD Almighty.* The first word, 'Behold' (omitted in some translations), is important as it draws attention to the important statement that will follow. This is a well-known introduction to a judgment oracle where doom is announced upon nations with the terrible threat that YHWH himself will enter into the battle to defeat the enemy once and for all.

For a woman to have her nakedness exposed by having her *skirts* lifted up *over [her] face*, thereby exposing the whole of her body, was a punishment for adultery but also an utter humiliation. This terrible humiliation will be on public display for all the nations and kingdoms to see. Added to the sexual humiliation is the statement that she (the city) will be covered with dirt (*filth*) and as a result will be treated with *contempt* and made *a spectacle*. The inevitable conclusion people will draw as a consequence of this public spectacle that was once the capital of the Assyrian Empire is that this city is now devastated. Because of the cruel treatment others received from Nineveh, she will now not receive any *comfort* from anybody. There is a clever play on words in verse 7: the name of the prophet means 'comforter', yet there will be no comfort for the Assyrians.

However, this message of the total devastation of the Assyrians is a comforting one to the people of God.

8–10. Verse 8 is an important verse in the book as it mentions No-Amon (Thebes), reminding the people of what happened to this city when it was conquered by Assyria in 663 BC. This historical reference provides us with at least a *terminus a quo* for dating the book (cf. the Introduction). All of a sudden, the reader is confronted with a series of names of cities and countries: *Thebes* (No-Amon), *Cush* (Ethiopia), *Egypt*, *Put* and *Libya* (or Lubin). A rhetorical question is asked, in expectation of the answer 'No': Nineveh can in no way be regarded as better than the city of No-Amon. The Hebrew text reads *nō'-'āmôn*, meaning 'city of (the god) Amon'. Amon was known as the sun-god and the chief god of Egypt. Thebes (cf. Jer. 46:25; Ezek. 30:14–16) was the Greek name of the city situated on the River Nile which was the capital of Egypt during much of the second and first millennia BC. Its location, surrounded by water, acted as a natural defence. Having *water around her* probably refers to a system of canals in the Nile which provided protection for the city. The area south of Egypt was known as *Cush* (now Ethiopia) and was under Egyptian rule at that time. Lubin, or *Libya,* can be found to the west of Egypt, but the location of *Put* is uncertain. All of these cities and countries were allies of Egypt. Eventually, Thebes was conquered by Assyria under the leadership of Ashurbanipal in 663 BC and had to suffer the devastation and humiliation of being defeated by a superior military force in the most brutal manner. Not even the allies mentioned could be of any help when Thebes was besieged by the Assyrian army. The point that the prophet wants to make is clear: there is historical proof that even strong cities of seemingly invincible power eventually come to an end, suffering the same fate they once meted out to others. To compare the fate of Thebes to what will happen to Nineveh is apt. Both cities relied on water for protection from foreign invaders (cf. 2:6, 8), and now Nineveh, the city that once conquered Thebes, will suffer the same fate as Thebes at the hand of Nineveh. To put the message in a nutshell: just as Thebes fell, so will Nineveh fall. The message to the people of God is that ultimately it is not the superpowers of the day that are in control of world events, but rather YHWH, the God of Israel.

11–14. The verb used in verse 11 means to *become drunk*. In 1:10 it was also said that Nineveh will become drunk from the wine they drink. The imagery of being drunk suggests that the inhabitants of Nineveh will drink the cup of God's wrath, leaving them vulnerable and unable to defend themselves against the enemy. Weakened by drinking from the cup of wrath, they will seek a place to hide from an invading enemy. The once-mighty Assyrian military force will no longer be in a position to attack others and conquer territory; instead, it will now have to flee and seek refuge from the enemies attacking it. A complete reversal of fortunes is foreseen. In the next metaphor, the fortified cities built to protect the citizens (or possibly the fortifications at the walls and gates of Nineveh) are likened to *fig-trees* bearing fruit ready to be taken and devoured by the people that pass by. The idea conveyed is that, just as ripe figs falling from the tree are ready to eat without much effort (*figs fall into the mouth of the eater!*), so it will be easy for the invading army to conquer Nineveh.

In verse 13 the mighty, ruthless, brave and fearless Assyrian soldiers are insulted by being compared to 'women' (NRSV; NIV *weaklings*). Clearly this is meant as yet another way of humiliating the city of Nineveh together with all the inhabitants of the Assyrian Empire. Keeping in mind that this insult comes from a powerless and minute subdued people, it is daring to say the least. Comparison of a weak army to women is found elsewhere in the Old Testament: in Isaiah 19:16 the Egyptians are compared to women, while in Jeremiah 50:37 and 51:30 it is the Babylonians – a comparison that could be made in a male-dominated society where women were seen as inferior to men. The consequence of having such a weakened army is that the *gates* will be without any defence and therefore open to an invading army. To make matters even worse, the *bars* used to lock the gates have already been set on fire.

Verse 14 is an ironic call to battle. Even though the army is already weakened and the gates are already open to an invading military force, it now has to prepare for war. The army has to secure an adequate supply of water; its fortifications have to be strengthened to withstand the onslaught of the coming enemy; and an already decaying city will have to be restored.

15–17. Verse 15 introduces *locusts* as a new metaphor. Despite the (futile) preparations named in verse 14, the inhabitants of the city will be devoured by *fire* and the *sword will cut* them off. Just as an entire crop in the fields can be devoured by a swarm of locusts, so the Assyrians will be devoured by foreign military forces, with nothing left. Even if the Assyrians manage to increase their numbers as locusts do, it will be of no help. It might be that there is 'safety in numbers', but in the final and decisive battle, the size of the population and the multitude of soldiers will be of no help to the Assyrians. It is at once apparent that the metaphor of locusts is applied differently in these verses: in the first part of verse 15 it is locusts' ability to devastate crops in fields ready for harvest that is the point of comparison; in the second part of the verse it is their ability to multiply to such an extent that their numbers are beyond human control. In the first instance it is the invading army that is compared to a swarm of locusts, and in the second instance it is the invaded people, emphasizing their ability to multiply. The *merchants* mentioned in verse 16 probably refers to the people who managed to profit from the oppressed nations in business deals, hence the reference to locusts who *strip the land*. It may also be that at the moment the Assyrian Empire was threatened by another army, the merchants just took off to a safer place to hide themselves and their accumulated wealth. The *guards* and *officials* who are supposed to defend the people from foreign threats will flee, never to be seen again.

18–19. With verse 18 there is a slight change in tone. The last two verses do not give a description of the fall of Nineveh as in the previous verses, but rather celebrate the defeat of the king and the city. It is interesting to note that the king of Assyria is addressed in particular. In contrast to the activity suggested in the previous verses through the use of the locusts metaphor, here the *shepherds* are asleep and the *nobles lie down to rest*. *Shepherds* refers to the rulers within the Assyrian Empire who assist the king in leading his subjects. They are now asleep and are therefore useless. It is possible that the mention of the rulers sleeping serves a double duty and refers also to their deaths, with sleep being used metaphorically to indicate death. It is also an indication that the king has lost control of his subjects. Instead of serving the king by fulfilling their duties on his behalf for the benefit of the people, the rulers are asleep, with no regard for the king. The king is unable to provide leadership, with the result that the people are *scattered on the mountains*, apparently fleeing for dear life, with no-one to lead them and bring them together again. The king's empire has suffered a fatal wound without any hope of recovery. The Assyrian Empire is personified in the king; hence the *wound* that is *fatal* for the king means that the empire is fatally wounded. The *news* of the king's being fatally wounded is met with joy and jubilation by the many who have had to suffer from his cruel rule.

The book concludes with a rhetorical question: *who has not felt your endless cruelty?* The only other book that ends with a rhetorical question is Jonah: 'should I not have concern for the great city of Nineveh . . . ?' (Jon. 4:11). This can hardly be a coincidence as both books deal with the city of Nineveh as the capital of the Assyrian Empire. The contrast couldn't be more apparent. In the case of Nahum, doom is pronounced on Nineveh. In the case of Jonah, redemption is proclaimed to Nineveh by the unwilling prophet. In the book of Nahum, it is God's justice that prevails; in the book of Jonah, it is God's mercy. Jonah was likely written many years after Nahum, so it may be concluded that in the end YHWH's mercy triumphs over his judgment.

Meaning

What is the theological message of this last chapter? Nineveh will be invaded by an enemy that will overpower it. The city is compared to a prostitute and a wicked woman to indicate its utter humiliation. What is more, history will prove the prophecy to be true because what will happen to Nineveh has happened before. The city will be weakened, ready to be invaded, like ripe figs falling from the fig tree. Attempts to defend the city will be futile and the inhabitants will have no other option than to flee. It is almost unthinkable that the once-invincible Assyria will now have to flee from an invading enemy. What is the theological purpose of a pronouncement of doom and destruction like this?

This chapter (and in fact the book as a whole) makes it clear that God is in control of world events. God is not only God of his people; he is God of the world. It is YHWH who is against Assyria

(Nah. 3:5) and it is he who will bring humiliation upon them. The fact that the army that will invade and conquer Assyria is never mentioned by name indicates that it is YHWH who will bring Assyria down. What happened once to No-Amon (Thebes) will happen to Nineveh. As also seen in the rest of the book, the people of God will be mere spectators of what is about to happen; Judah will have no role to play in the eventual downfall of Nineveh and the Assyrian Empire. This conviction that God is in control of world powers is strengthened in this chapter.

The prophecy of the imminent demise of Nineveh is also intended to foster hope. When nations have to suffer under the brutalities of a totalitarian regime like the Assyrian Empire, the people may despair. Is it possible that a mighty power like the Assyrians will ever fall? Yet in language that actually taunts the enemy, it is prophesied that this cruel rule of the Assyrian Empire will come to an end. In this way, hope is given to people in a seemingly hopeless situation. By giving them this hope, Nahum, true to his name, brings comfort to his people. Thus, Assyria and its capital refer here to more than simply a world power sometime during the seventh century BC; they become a symbol of all oppressive political powers that take away other people's freedom and dignity. Indeed, Assyria was not the last oppressive power to rule the world. Yet all nations that follow Assyria also eventually fall, even when it seems impossible. And, as was the case for Assyria, when tyrants fall it is met with joy and jubilation. Today we can see on our TV screens the joy and celebration among people who have been freed from oppressive rulers. During such times of oppression, then, those who suffer need not lose hope. The people of God of all times may find hope in the prophecy of Nahum that evil world powers will come to an end. It happened in the case of Assyria and has happened many times since. It is hope that gives people the resilience to endure present suffering. Is life possible without hope?

HABAKKUK

INTRODUCTION

1. The prophet Habakkuk

Virtually nothing is known about Habakkuk, the person behind the prophetic book that bears his name. His name appears twice in two headings in the book (1:1; 3:1) where he is simply introduced as Habakkuk the prophet. His name does not appear anywhere else in the Old Testament and we have no other information about him. Where did he come from? Was he married? Did he have children? Did he have another occupation, like Amos the farmer? We do not know what age he was when he engaged in this intense dialogue with God, and we have no information about what happened to him after this encounter. The superscription does not provide the reader with any information about the date and historical time frame of the book either.

Although nothing is known of the prophet, the style and vocabulary used in the book, suggesting a liturgical nature, may indicate that Habakkuk was closely associated with the temple; he is therefore sometimes seen as a kind of cult prophet. From

1 Chronicles 25:1 we know that staff members working in the temple did utter prophecies with lyres, harps (stringed instruments, as indicated in Hab. 3:19a) and cymbals. The complaints as well as the eventual prayer are associated with the Psalms that reflect a close connection to the temple. Habakkuk is also very familiar with the main traditions of Israel, telling the history of God's acts of deliverance in the past.

Perhaps because of this lack of knowledge about the prophet himself, the figure of Habakkuk has given rise to legends. Some rabbis were of the opinion that he was the son of the Shunammite woman (2 Kgs 4:16), while another theory within rabbinic circles held that he was the watchman referred to in Isaiah 21:6 because Habakkuk once stood on a watchtower (Hab. 2:1). In one of the additions to the book of Daniel (Bel and the Dragon) Habakkuk was brought by an angel to Daniel in the lions' den to provide him with food he had prepared to take to harvesters in the fields of Judah. Of course, none of these legends have any historical value.

2. Dating the book

Having some idea of when a prophetic book originated is vital to a better understanding of the book. Knowing the historical context of Old Testament books is important for gaining a valid interpretation, especially because we are separated from these writings by centuries. In the case of Habakkuk there is only one reference to a historical event that may assist current readers to read the book within a specific historical context. In 1:6 mention is made of the Babylonians:

> *I am raising up the Babylonians,*
> *that ruthless and impetuous people.*

When this reference to the Babylonians (the *Kashdim* in Hebrew) is taken as a point of orientation regarding the dating of the book, the end of the seventh century BC seems likely. From about 625 BC the Neo-Babylonian Empire started to gain power under the leadership of Nabopolasser, the founder of the Chaldean dynasty, when he succeeded in establishing Babylon as an independent city-state from the Assyrian Empire. In 612 BC Nineveh, the capital of the Assyrian Empire, was demolished, but it was only after the decisive victory over King Neco of Egypt at Carchemish in 605 BC that the Babylonians became the next superpower of that time. With the Babylonian Empire in power, the reign of the Assyrian Empire that had begun in 745 BC came to an end. With King Neco forced to retreat to Egypt, the whole of Syria and Palestine was now subjected to Babylonian control.

If this historical reconstruction holds true, then a probable date for the book is between 605 BC (as the start of Babylonian dominance) and 597 BC (as the date of the first deportation of Judeans into Babylonian exile). It is clear that the setting of the book is indeed the years after the Babylonians came to power but before the deportation of Judeans into exile in Babylonia. In 2:20 the temple is mentioned still as the earthly dwelling of YHWH, with no hint whatsoever that it may be or has been destroyed by the Babylonian forces. It is also highly unlikely that the temple that was rebuilt during Persian rule (516/515 BC) is meant in 2:20. The content of the book was probably written down sometime during the Babylonian exile when it became apparent that what had been foreseen in Habakkuk had actually become reality with the invasion of Judah and the exile to Babylonia. It is also noteworthy that no king is mentioned by name, even though the last of the Judean kings played a part in the eventual downfall of Judah as an independent state.

The last kings of Judah were part of world history as it unfolded in the demise of Assyrian rule and the rise of the Neo-Babylonian Empire. While the Assyrian Empire weakened, Josiah (640–609 BC) became king and Judah was for all practical purposes an independent country. King Josiah took advantage of this situation and introduced a number of reforms to align the people once again with the stipulations of (at least some parts of) the book of Deuteronomy. When the Egyptian king Neco (609–593 BC) supported the Assyrians, Josiah acted against him but was killed at Megiddo during the battle. Jehoahaz became king in his place. Jehoahaz, however, was king for only three months before he was deported and imprisoned in Egypt. Eliakim, the brother of Jehoahaz, became the next king, but he was a mere vassal of Egypt and his name was changed to Jehoiakim. The conditions described by

Jeremiah 22:13–19 fit well with the first complaint of Habakkuk in 1:2–4. With the defeat of the Egyptian forces at Carchemish in 605 BC by the hand of Nebuchadnezzar, Jehoiakim became an unwilling vassal of Babylon. He took the fatal decision to rebel against Nebuchadnezzar, and Nebuchadnezzar retaliated. Jehoiakim died in December 589 BC and his son Jehoiachin succeeded him. Jerusalem had to surrender within three months and Jehoiachin, the queen mother and other officials, along with a great amount of booty, were taken to Babylon. Zedekiah, the uncle of the king, was appointed ruler in Judah while Jehoiachin was still acknowledged king of Judah. When nationalism sparked another rebellion, the Babylonian king acted with force, besieged Jerusalem (587/586 BC), devastated the temple and took the blinded Zedekiah to Babylon, where he died (2 Kgs 25:6; Jer. 52:9–11). Judah suffered dearly: the Davidic dynasty came to an end, they lost the land promised and granted to them, and the temple was demolished. The Babylonians ruled until 539 BC, when the Persian Empire under the leadership of Cyrus became the next world power.

One of the most extreme proposals in terms of dating the book came from Bernard Duhm, who in 1906 dated the book to the fourth century BC. He emended the *Kashdim* (Chaldeans) to *Kittim*, referring to the Greeks and the campaigns of Alexander the Great. Although other scholars (Herrmann 2001: 481–496; Witte 2009: 67–91) also think in terms of a date in the early Hellenistic period, most scholars are still convinced that a late seventh-century date is the most appropriate one for the book of Habakkuk.

3. Literary issues

a. The literary unity of the book
One of the burning issues in the research on the book is the problem of its literary unity. Given the different style and character of chapter 3, the question whether this chapter belonged to the original composition has been a matter of discussion. In the Qumran manuscripts written as a *pesher* (IQpHab) on the book of Habakkuk there is commentary on only the first two chapters; chapter 3 is omitted. This has given rise to the question whether the last chapter of the book should be viewed as a later addition. It has been argued that

the last verse of chapter 2 can be viewed as a perfect ending to the book: after all the complaints voiced by the prophet have been answered extensively by YHWH in chapter 2, and the book concludes that it is now best to be silent in the awesome presence of YHWH in his temple. A second argument is that the style and literary genre used in chapter 3 is totally different from that in the first two chapters. However, that Habakkuk 3 is not included in the Qumran manuscript on the book is not a conclusive argument that the last chapter was not part of the book. Another Hebrew manuscript consisting of the Minor Prophets dating from more or less the same time as IQpHab does contain chapter 3 of Habakkuk (Haak 1992: 3). Chapter 3 continues the dialogical style of the first two chapters, such that it can be viewed not only as the continuation of the dialogue but also as the conclusion and climax of the book. It should also be noted that chapter 3 is part of the book in all of the LXX manuscripts as well as in a number of texts from the third and second centuries BC (Baker 1988: 46). Furthermore, there are several semantic and syntactical links between chapter 3 and the preceding chapters that will be highlighted in the commentary. Even if it is possible that chapter 3 was a later addition to the book, it was added in such a skilful way that the end product can still be seen as a literary unit, taking the reader from the initial complaints of the prophet to the climax of a confession of faith and a renewed trust in God.

b. Literary genres used

A variety of literary genres are used in the book. The headings for the two main parts of the book (1:1 and 3:1) indicate the genres used as being a prophetic announcement in 1:2 – 2:20 and a psalm of complaint in 3:1–19. Other literary genres found in the first part of the book are the complaints of the prophet (1:2–4, 12–17) and the woe oracles (2:5–19); and in the second part of the book, a psalm of complaint or lament (3:1–19). The occurrence of different genres does not necessarily point to multiple authorship. A single author may make use of more than one literary genre.

c. Textual issues

Scholars are in agreement that although the Hebrew text of the book is not in perfect condition, it is in a relatively good condition.

In the commentary section some areas of difficulty in understanding the text will be discussed.

4. An outline of the theological message of Habakkuk

The book offers a rich harvest of theological insights.

God is portrayed as the Lord of world history. He is capable of
doing the impossible, such as

> *raising up the Babylonians,*
>   *that ruthless and impetuous people*
> (1:6)

to act against the injustices, destruction and violence, strife and
conflict characteristic of his people (1:2–4). The woe oracles (2:5–19)
are further evidence of God's power to control world affairs and to
act against any nation. In chapter 3 God is presented as the God
who reveals himself in a theophany in which his sheer power and
might are simply overwhelming.

God is portrayed as the God of justice. God's answer to the
initial complaint of the prophet is indicative of the fact that God
cares about justice and righteousness. Justice and righteousness are
the pillars of human society. Because God is the Lord of world
history, injustices beyond the boundaries of Judah are also his
concern. Therefore the injustices of foreign nations are brought
to light and they are judged for their greed, plunder, bloodshed,
crime, violence and general disregard for human dignity. There
is no conflict between ethics and religion in this book. Injustices
and violence brought about by human beings in any society are un-
acceptable, and because God is the God of justice he is approached
to act upon this state of affairs.

God is portrayed as the God of mercy. Habakkuk is allowed to
voice his questions, discomfort and perhaps even anger against
God. Never in the book is Habakkuk reprimanded for questioning God and his actions or his apparent lack of action. In 3:2
the prophet calls upon YHWH to remember his mercy when he is
about to judge the wicked. The prophet is also well aware of
YHWH's acts of deliverance in the history of his people, when the

people experienced his mercy time and again. In fact, the prophet's prayer is that YHWH's deeds in the past may be renewed in his time.

The book also addresses the issue of theodicy. Habakkuk asks the age-old question, 'Why, God?' The answer that Habakkuk gets is a complicated one. The first part of the answer is that human beings are incapable of understanding God's ways of handling world affairs. When God reveals to Habakkuk that he is about to raise up the Babylonians in response to his complaint, Habakkuk finds it simply incomprehensible. The prophet's attention was focused on the situation in Judah, but God widens his perspective to a worldwide vision. That solution to the problem is, according to the prophet, no solution at all. It is just not possible or sensible for violence and injustice to be rectified by more violence and injustice. Yet even when Habakkuk confronts God, taking him up on this matter, the answer remains the same (2:5–20). The second part of the answer is that the righteous must keep faith, even in the trying times they are living through. Over against the wicked who will not endure, the righteous will live through faith.

God's response is in no way a direct answer to Habakkuk's complaint. Habakkuk's question was 'Why, God?' and God's answer is 'Keep faith'. God does not provide Habakkuk with an explanation as to why the Babylonians will be the next world power and why injustices and violence will be met with more injustices and violence. The question of theodicy is answered but in a different way from what Habakkuk expected.

The book of Habakkuk reminds believing human beings that the way in which God directs world history is not revealed to us, nor can we comprehend God's control of history. In the end very little is said about the fate of the righteous in these troubled times. The answer that Habakkuk receives is actually quite vague. The prophet is reassured that YHWH is not inactive but will act against the injustices the prophet has observed. Yet the way in which YHWH will do that is out of line with what the prophet expected. To wait upon YHWH is another important theme in the book. After his second complaint the prophet awaits the response of YHWH (2:1), and in 3:16 he declares that he

will wait patiently for the day of calamity
to come on the nation invading us.

In the interim, before the prophecy is fulfilled, the righteous must keep faith because ultimately the injustices will be overcome. In a strange way, the vague answer proves to be enough for the prophet. He yields to the superior power of YHWH and his complaints turn to a joyous confession of faith and renewed trust in God at the end of the book, even though the hard times persist.

Habakkuk 2:4 is a crucial verse in the book, especially verse 4b where it is stated that the righteous shall live by faith – a verse which is taken up in the New Testament in the letters to the Romans (1:17), Galatians (3:11) and Hebrews (10:38). The Hebrew word used for *faith* (*'ĕmûnâ*) indicates a wide range of possible meanings: firmness, fidelity, steadfastness, trustworthiness, faith, faithfulness. On the one hand, believers are encouraged to keep faith by trusting the message conveyed to the prophet, while on the other hand, they are also encouraged to be faithful to the Lord by living according to the covenant stipulations. Within the context of the book it is the only verse that addresses the fate of the righteous. The rest of the book is more about God's justice that will prevail against the wicked and those responsible for the injustices and violence the prophet has complained about. In the New Testament, especially in the Pauline letters, the verse is interpreted as 'the one who is righteous by faith will live', meaning that believers are justified by faith alone. Life according to the Pauline interpretation means trusting God and the promises he has made, rather than trusting in one's own achievements and abilities.

ANALYSIS

The book of Habakkuk is known for its dialogical structure. The prophet enters into a dialogue with YHWH in which he voices his discomfort with the current conditions in his country and YHWH responds to the prophet's complaints. The book falls into two clearly marked parts introduced by a superscription: Habakkuk 1 – 2 and Habakkuk 3.

    A. The superscription to the book (1:1)
    B. Two complaints by the prophet Habakkuk and two responses from YHWH (1:2 – 2:20)
        i. The first complaint of Habakkuk (1:2–4)
        ii. YHWH's response (1:5–11)
        iii. The second complaint of Habakkuk (1:12 – 2:1)
        iv. YHWH's second response (2:2–20)
            a. To live by faith even in times of adversity (2:2–5)
            b. The woe oracles (2:6–20)
    C. The prayer-cum-psalm of the prophet Habakkuk (3:1–19)
        i. Superscription (3:1)
        ii. The prophet calls upon YHWH (3:2)
        iii. The coming of YHWH (3:3–7)

COMMENTARY

A. The superscription to the book (1:1)

Context

The brief heading to the book provides the reader with little but important information. First of all, this prophetic book is introduced to the reader as a *prophecy*, or 'oracle'. The noun used is also found in the other prophetic books of the Old Testament (Isa. 13:1; 14:28; 15:1; 17:1; 19:1; 21:1, 11, 13; 22:1; 23:1; 30:6; Ezek. 12:10; Nah. 1:1; Zech. 9:1; 12:1; Mal. 1:1). The noun also has the notion of 'burden' or 'load', suggesting that the oracle is a kind of a burden upon the prophet that must be delivered. The noun can also be rendered as 'message', 'announcement' or 'proclamation'.

Comment

1. This oracle or message was *received* by Habakkuk. In the original Hebrew it is stated that the oracle was 'seen', presumably in the form of a vision by Habakkuk. The oracle was therefore not something thought out by the prophet – it was a message he received, something revealed to him. The oracle or message should be read and heard as divine revelation. The person to whom the oracle was revealed is identified as *Habakkuk the prophet*. The exact meaning of the name *Habakkuk* is not certain. Jerome and Luther related the name to a term that can be rendered 'the one who embraces' or 'embracer'. Another, more recent theory is that the name can be traced to the name of a plant, perhaps something like a cucumber (Rudolph 1975: 199). Naming human beings after plants is not that uncommon; Tamar (meaning 'palm') serves as an example. Nothing else is known about the prophet. We do not know where he was born or came from, who his father was, whether or not he was married, or for how long or at what time he acted as a prophet in Judean society; nor is there any account of his calling to be a prophet. He is finally identified as *the prophet*. A prophet is a spokesperson for God. His being announced as *the prophet* may be an indication that he was known in society as a prophet. In Habakkuk 3:1 he is once again referred to as *Habakkuk the prophet*. There is an interesting connection between being a prophet and 'seeing' an oracle – according to 1 Samuel 9:9 a prophet was formerly known as a 'seer'.

Meaning
The first verse provides the reader of the book with important pointers in terms of what to expect when reading further. The book has to be seen as an oracle divinely revealed to a prophet. The prophet is a human being known by his name but at the same time also a messenger of God. God revealed himself and his will through human beings.

B. Two complaints by the prophet Habakkuk and two responses from YHWH (1:2 – 2:20)

i. The first complaint of Habakkuk (1:2–4)
Context
Habakkuk 1:2 marks the start of the first unit in the book. This new unit is distinguished from the superscription by the questions posed (*How long... ?* in v. 2 and *Why... ?* in v. 3). Verse 4 brings the unit to a close with the conclusion introduced by *Therefore*. The unit is characterized by the occurrence of several word pairs: 'evil' and 'trouble' (or *injustice* and *wrongdoing*, NIV) (v. 3); *destruction* and *violence* (v. 3); *strife* and *conflict* (v. 3); *law* and *justice* (v. 4); and finally an antithetic word pair: *the wicked* and *the righteous* (v. 4) (Prinsloo 1989: 75–77). The occurrence of first-person singular forms together with second-person singular forms serves as an introduction to the dialogical structure characteristic of the book as a whole. The prophet enters into a dialogue with YHWH.

Comment
2–3. The unit commences with a complaint (Robertson 1990: 137; Sweeney 1991: 66; Haak 1992: 30) or lament (Roberts 1991: 88).

The complaint bears a striking resemblance to the complaints of individuals often found in the book of Psalms (4:2; 6:3; 13:1; 35:17; 62:3; 74:10; 79:5; 80:4; 82:2; 90:13; 94:3).

The questions imply that the intolerable situation the prophet describes has been going on for a considerable period of time. On more than one occasion in the past the prophet called to the Lord, but apparently to no avail. The words used (*call, cry out*) suggest a degree of urgency, an intensity of dire need, on the side of the prophet. The prophet cries out to YHWH but he does not *listen*, nor does he come to *save* his people. This situation is in contrast to what the people of God have experienced in the past. Once when YHWH heard their cry (Exod. 3:7) he responded with the miraculous deliverance from the bondage in Egypt. These questions are directed to the same God who once rescued them from Egypt, YHWH, the covenant God of Israel/Judah.

On the one hand, the issue of *destruction and violence* is addressed, but on the other hand, YHWH is asked why he does not act against the *destruction and violence*. The word *violence* occurs twice and can therefore be seen as the main complaint of the prophet. This raises the question of what kind of violence he is referring to. One possibility is that the prophet is thinking of the violence of foreign powers like the Assyrians or the Babylonians. However, it is improbable that foreign powers are meant here. At the time of the prophet the Assyrians were no longer a threat, as they had been defeated by 612 BC. It is also unlikely that the Babylonians are meant because they will come into play in the next unit (1:5–11). Another, more probable possibility is that the *destruction and violence*, *strife* and *conflict* refer to the situation within the people of God in Judah. The terminology points in the direction of the situation within Judah itself. The reference to the *law* (Torah) being *paralysed* and *justice* not prevailing (v. 4) is typical Old Testament language. The word pair *destruction and violence* is also one found often in the prophetical literature of the Old Testament to criticize social injustices in the community of the covenant people (Isa. 60:18; Jer. 6:7; 20:8; Ezek. 45:9; Amos 3:9).

4. Verse 4 draws a conclusion introduced by *Therefore*. Destruction and violence, strife and conflict are characteristic of society because the Torah has become numb or *paralysed* and *justice* is not seen any more. Justice in particular is practised within the realm of human relationships, but the prophet concludes that *wicked* people now surround *the righteous*, with *justice* being *perverted*. Just as violence was mentioned twice, so justice is also mentioned twice in verse 4, emphasizing the gravity of the situation.

Meaning
The real issue raised by the prophet is not simply the occurrence of violence and destruction, but that YHWH does not act to remedy the situation. The emphasis is not on those who have committed the violence but rather on YHWH who is apparently absent and therefore ignorant of the plight of (especially) the righteous people living in the land. YHWH is known to be the God of justice, so in the apparent absence of justice a serious theological question arises: where is YHWH, the God of justice?

ii. YHWH's response (1:5–11)
Context
The next unit is understood as YHWH's response to the complaint raised by Habakkuk, although we have no direct evidence that it is indeed YHWH who answers Habakkuk's complaint. The imperatives (*Look*, *watch*, 'wonder/marvel', 'be astonished' [NRSV]) used in verse 5, however, indicate a change in who is speaking and suggest that it is no longer the prophet uttering his complaint. Verses 5–11 are also marked by third-person singular forms in contrast to the first- and second-person singular forms found in 1:2–4. In verse 12 YHWH is addressed in the vocative, marking a distinction from 1:5–11 and clearly indicating that it is the prophet speaking in reaction to what has been revealed to him in the previous verses.

Comment
5–7. YHWH is going to act against the violence and destruction, the powerlessness of the Torah and the injustices in society mentioned in the prophet's complaint, and in a remarkable way. He is going to do something astonishing, so astonishing that people will find it difficult to believe when they are told about it. YHWH's reaction will be the cause for wonder and amazement, and will be met as something utterly incredible (Snyman 2003: 425). The

prophet's complaint was about the social conditions within the covenant people, but verse 5 opens up a wider horizon as the nations beyond the borders of Judah are to be observed. Whereas the prophet had looked and seen the evil and all that was wrong within Judean society, he and the people are now summoned to *Look* and *watch* what YHWH is about to let happen. The scope is widened from Habakkuk's local interest to the scene of world history. It is interesting to note that the same verbs are used in verses 3 and 5. YHWH's action is imminent as this extraordinary event will take place *in your days*. The initial complaint of the prophet, *How long, LORD . . . ?*, is thus answered.

The surprising act of YHWH is stated in verse 6,[1] introduced by the Hebrew particle *kî, For*. He is going to raise up the Chaldeans, also known as the *Babylonians*. A foreign power is going to be an instrument in the hands of YHWH to act against the injustices Habakkuk has complained about. The Babylonians are described in rather vicious terms: they are a nation that is bitter (or *ruthless*) and *impetuous*, and they simply march *across the earth* and *seize dwellings* that do not belong to them. The Babylonians were formerly under the control of the previous dominating world power, Assyria, but matters changed within a few years. The Assyrians were defeated with the destruction of Nineveh in 612 BC and a few years later, in 605 BC, the Babylonian army overpowered the Egyptians at Carchemish on the Euphrates to become the next world power. The Babylonian power is further described in verse 7 as terrifying (to be *feared*) and frightful (terrible or dreadful; *dreaded*). The collapsed justice complained about by the prophet will be replaced by the justice of the Chaldeans as defined by *themselves* (Snyman 2003: 427).

8–9. The coming Babylonian army is described in verses 8–9 by means of metaphors taken from the animal world. Their *horses* are compared to *leopards* and *wolves*. Leopards and wolves are both predators known for their cruelty and cunning hunting skills. One should keep in mind that in Old Testament times human beings

---

1. For the importance of this verse in terms of the historical situation of the book of Habakkuk, cf. the Introduction.

were particularly vulnerable to predators. The metaphor of predators is used, then, to instil fear of the coming Babylonian army that will hunt people down as predators hunt their prey. In another metaphor the Babylonian army is compared to *an eagle* – a bird of prey – eager to devour its prey hastily by ripping it to pieces. The image of an eagle fits the point of the metaphor better than that of a vulture as is sometimes suggested, as vultures feed on animals already dead while eagles prey on live animals. A key element in addition to the predatory nature of the animals used in these metaphors is the notion of speed. The horses are likened to swift leopards, and eagles are known for their speed in flying, swooping down to snatch up their prey. Great distances will therefore be no problem for the approaching military force as they will come swiftly *from afar*. In no time they will advance to pose a real threat to the small country of Judah.

The first part of verse 9 provides the reader with an apt summary of what they will do: *they come intent on violence*. Violence in society was the reason for the prophet's complaint in the previous unit. Now the disturbing news is that even more violence is on its way; YHWH's answer to violence is violence. The second part of verse 9 is difficult to understand due to uncertainties in the Hebrew text (van der Woude 1978: 23; Robertson 1990: 122; Haak 1992: 44). The animal metaphors are dropped and a vivid description of an attacking army occupying land and taking captives is given. The 'multitude of faces' (according to a literal reading of the Hebrew text) may be understood as the soldiers pressing forward away from their homeland and towards foreign countries (NIV *Their hordes advance*). The *prisoners* of war are so many that they are compared to *sand*. Baker (1988: 63) observes that the simile of sand is often used in the Old Testament in a positive sense as a blessing (Gen. 32:12; 41:49), but here it is used in a negative sense.

10–11. Once a territory has been occupied, the Babylonians *mock* the foreign kings and laugh at officials. The army also laughs at *fortified cities*, suggesting the ease with which they take cities; they simply heap up dust or soil and seize them. Having conquered the mighty empires of Assyria and Egypt, the kings of smaller kingdoms are no threat to them. If they could take the mighty city of Nineveh, other cities will be no problem. Verse 11 serves as a summary of the foregoing response of YHWH to the complaint of Habakkuk. The sweeping power of the Babylonians is compared to the *wind* as they relentlessly move on, capturing land and cities. The text suggests that as the wind changes its direction, so too the Babylonians may suddenly move in another direction from what was expected. The unit comes to an end on a hopeful note, however: in the end this fearless and terrible world power will be found *guilty* because its own power has become the god its people worship.

Meaning

This unit provides an awkward answer to the complaints of the prophet. The issues of violence and lack of justice mentioned in the prophet's initial complaint are addressed, but in a quite unexpected way. The delay in YHWH's response is answered – he will act and it will happen *in your days*, according to verse 5. The way in which YHWH will respond, however, is an utter surprise; in fact, it will be hard to believe when it becomes known. The violence complained about will be met with the violence of a foreign power identified as the Babylonians. The problem raised by the prophet is, then, by no means resolved. According to this unit, YHWH seems to be the instigator of even more violence, and that beyond the borders of Judah. The Babylonians are portrayed as a violent nation sweeping across the earth to capture other nations with brutal force and power. The only glimmer of hope is that in the end it seems that they will be found guilty because they will worship their own power as their god (v. 11). The paralysed law will not be restored, nor will the injustices committed be dealt with. Justice will still be perverted by violence and destruction – indeed, on a greater scale than has been the case up to now. This leads to a theological dilemma: the claim of the text is that YHWH reacts to the complaints of the prophet by raising up the Babylonians, yet when the actions of the Babylonians are described, rather than alleviate the situation of violence and injustices in society, it seems that the situation will get worse. On the one hand, this unit confirms that YHWH is indeed the God of justice. On the other hand, the way in which YHWH maintains justice by instigating even more injustice is incomprehensible, and consequently the answer does not satisfy the prophet.

iii. The second complaint of Habakkuk (1:12 – 2:1)

Context

The prophet is not satisfied with the answer given in the previous unit. Verse 12 is the start of a second complaint directed by the prophet to YHWH. The unit commences with a rhetorical question reminding one of the questions asked in the first unit. Whereas YHWH spoke in the second unit (1:5–11), the use of second-person pronouns and vocatives is a clear indication that he is now addressed by the prophet as in the first unit (1:2–4). The issue of justice raised in the first unit is once more taken up in this second complaint. The unit can be divided into two parts: 1:12–13 addresses God and 1:14–17 makes use of metaphors (as was the case in 1:5–11) to describe the plight of the people suffering under the tyranny of a foreign political power. The last verse in this unit (2:1) then serves as a transitional verse to the next unit, where YHWH speaks again. The attention of the prophet has shifted from the situation in Judah to the broader perspective opened up by YHWH in the previous unit.

Comment

12–13. The prophet appeals to the very character of God in voicing his dissatisfaction with the answer he has received. YHWH is God 'from of old' or *from everlasting*, the literal translation of the Hebrew. He is God from all eternity. The same thought is expressed in Psalm 90:2:

> Before the mountains were born
> > or you brought forth the whole world,
> > from everlasting to everlasting you are God.

Calling upon God as the God of all eternity is often employed in the Old Testament to refer to God's role as creator and master of the world (Deut. 33:27; Prov. 8:22–23; Isa. 40:12–17; 44:2) (Snyman 2003: 427; Sweeney 1991: 69). Verse 12 makes a second statement about God: he is also the *holy* God. The way in which this is expressed sounds strange. Translated literally it may be rendered 'my holy God'. The use of the first-person singular form makes this an expression of a personal kind. It is thus not only an 'objective'

statement, taken from tradition or conventional faith, it is an expression of the prophet's personal conviction about God. The
holiness of God is a theme found throughout the Old Testament
but it is an attribute of God especially emphasized in the book of
Leviticus. It denotes the idea of God as incomparable, as totally
other than human beings.

The next phrase (*we will never die*, NIV margin) presents the reader
with a problem. The sudden change from first-person singular
forms to the first-person plural seems awkward. The problem is
further complicated by the fact that this phrase is regarded as one
of the so-called *Tiqqune Sopherim*, the 'corrections of the scribes'.
The original text probably read 'you [second-person singular] do
not die' (cf. NIV). It is argued that this change in the text might have
been made because the mere thought that YHWH might die is
unthinkable and bordering on the blasphemous, hence the change
to the first-person plural 'we will not die'. If one accepts the
singular reading, the meaning of the phrase is that because YHWH
is the holy God of all eternity, he will not and cannot die. If one
accepts the plural reading, the meaning is that in the light of YHWH
being the eternal and holy God, his people will overcome the
current difficult time of oppression by a foreign political power,
together with the injustices that go with it. As both interpretations
make good sense, it is almost impossible to accept one and reject
the other. The middle road is to allow room for the ambivalence of
these two possible readings.

The last statement about God is made in the form of a parallelism where, in the first part, YHWH is affirmed as the one who
maintains justice by appointing the Babylonians as his instrument to re-establish justice. In the second part of the parallelism
YHWH is also portrayed as a rock who has 'established [the Babylonians] for punishment' (NRSV). To view YHWH as a rock is not
unfamiliar in the Old Testament. It is an image found in the
Psalms and also in the book of Deuteronomy (32:4). It conveys
the idea of stability and hence portrays God as the reliable God
from time immemorial, the one to be trusted as the guardian and
keeper of his people. The Babylonians were the ones established
by YHWH to carry out his punishment upon those who proved to
be guilty of the injustices the prophet had complained about.

What the prophet does is to appeal to his moral integrity (Floyd 2000: 118).

Verse 13 continues with a description of who YHWH is. The thrust of the statements made in verse 13 is that YHWH's inactivity in the face of so much injustice, evil, wickedness, destruction and strife is irreconcilable with who he is. What the Babylonians do as an instrument in the hands of YHWH simply does not match the prophet's concept of who God is and how he has acted in the course of history. The distance between YHWH's *pure eyes* and the *evil* is just too great to comprehend. The implication is that what YHWH sees, he also allows. It is inconceivable that YHWH should *tolerate* the *wrongdoing* that the prophet has to witness. In fact, it seems as if the problem will get worse because of the Babylonians, instead of getting better. The second part of verse 13 takes on a different tone, coming close to an accusation, when the prophet repeats his initial question put in verse 3: *Why . . . ?* Why does YHWH look upon the *treacherous* and remain *silent*? Why is it that wicked people *swallow up* righteous people? It seems as if the metaphor of an eagle devouring its prey in verse 8 is picked up again. According to the experience and observation of the prophet, God is acting contrary to his character and is therefore in conflict with his own being (van der Woude 1978: 28). How is it possible that a God of righteousness could replace one society with another even more idolatrous and evil (Achtemeier 1986: 40)?

14–17. As was done in the previous unit (v. 8), the prophet now makes use of metaphors to illustrate his dissatisfaction with YHWH's apparent inactivity. In verse 8 metaphors from the animal world on land and the birds in the sky were used. Here human beings are compared to fish and 'crawling' (NRSV) sea creatures. There is also a subtle change in tone that can be detected in this verse. It is no longer the Babylonians whose cruel acts are likened to leopards and wolves as in verse 8: the accusation is now directed towards YHWH himself. It is he who has treated people in an inhumane way. The creational order has been turned upside down. Human beings were entrusted 'to rule over the fish in the sea' (Gen. 1:26), but now humans are treated like fish. In Genesis 1 human beings were created in the image of God, but here human beings are likened to fish. Just as fish are vulnerable to being caught by humans without any real defence mechanism, so the people of God are vulnerable to the viciousness of the Babylonian army as an instrument in God's hand. The creatures in the sea *have no ruler*, as can be seen by the way in which they swim in the sea. As a result, they are also without anyone to guard them. Likewise, humans are vulnerable and an easy target for the overwhelming military force of a foreign power like the Babylonians.

In verse 15 the fish metaphor is now applied to what the Babylonians do. They catch people making use of *hooks* and then gather them up in nets. There is evidence of prisoners of war being taken in nets (van der Woude 1978: 29; Robertson 1990: 122; Haak 1992: 44). It is also known that the Babylonians drove a hook through the sensitive lower lip of their captives to string them in single file (Robertson 1990: 162). The image of fish being caught is not an unfamiliar one in the Old Testament when depicting a conqueror (Jer. 16:16; Ezek. 12:13; Amos 4:2). Once a fish has been caught in a net there is no way for it to escape and death is certain. In a similar way, the weaker nations do not have any way of escaping the superior military power of the Babylonians. This gives the Babylonians more than enough reason to *rejoice* and be *glad* as they are the ultimate victors on the world scene. It is also interesting to note that in the previous unit, the metaphor of predators attacking their prey with amazing speed was used from the perspective of the Babylonians, while in this unit the perspective has changed to the victims of the hunt. Human beings are treated like fish caught by hooks and nets.

Just as in the previous unit (1:11), this unit draws to an end with a religious perspective. The fishing tackle used to capture people is worshipped with sacrifices and incense. It is the Babylonians' own skill and know-how in making the best use of their weapons that secures success. In verse 11 it was their power that was acknowledged as their god; here it is their superior military might that is honoured in a religious way. It is all about the deification of military power and strength.

2:1. The unit concludes in 2:1 with Habakkuk awaiting YHWH's response to his second complaint. Habakkuk 2:1 forms a kind of interlude in the book. While the verse serves as a conclusion to the complaint of the prophet, it is also a bridge to the following section where YHWH will answer the complaints of the prophet in more detail. The first part of verse 1 is structured in a chiastic way: (A) On my watch-post (B) I shall stand and (B') I shall station myself (A') on my watchtower. The image is clearly that of a sentinel looking out for a message or messenger of some kind to arrive. It is not certain whether the watch-post has a military or cultic background. There is no indication from the text that a place near the temple is meant. This is also not an unfamiliar image in prophetic literature. In Isaiah 21:6–9 the prophet stands on a watchtower waiting expectantly for news of the fall of Babylon. In Ezekiel 3:17–21 the prophet Ezekiel is 'made . . . a watchman for the people of Israel' to 'give them warning from me' (Ezek. 3:17). To be on the lookout also has the nuance of 'waiting upon' (Bratcher 1984: 108). In 1 Samuel 4:13 Eli was 'sitting on his chair by the side of the road, watching, because his heart feared for the ark of God'. The prophet, then, takes up a position of watching and waiting for a response from God. It is not clear from the text whether a real or metaphorical watch-post is meant.

The notion of 'seeing' is important. The superscription to the book indicated that Habakkuk 'saw' the oracle he has to deliver; in 1:3 he 'looked' at the injustices committed in society; and in 1:5 God broadened the prophet's perspective by telling him to 'look' at the nations. Now the prophet waits to 'see' what will be revealed to him. Habakkuk is not satisfied with the initial answer he has received and consequently he has dared to question God further on this matter. The prophet continues to wait patiently for an answer from YHWH.

Meaning

The nagging question the prophet has is still not answered and the unit comes to an end voicing it once again. Will this violent way of destroying nations continue without any demonstration of mercy or pity? In fact, the situation has worsened. It is no longer only a question of God being inactive and passive in view of so much injustice, as the prophet initially thought in his first complaint (1:2–4). Rather, it now seems that YHWH is actively involved in world affairs, restoring justice but doing so by making use of the Babylonian forces in a strange and incomprehensible way that amounts to even harsher injustice, making the situation worse rather than better, thus heightening the tension. There is also tension on another level: between the prophet's understanding of who God is and what he does, and the reality of the Babylonians acting the way they do. The answer given has not resolved the matter; on the contrary, the initial problem is intensified.

Perhaps that is exactly the important point not to overlook in the book of Habakkuk. The way in which God exercises his control of world events as they play themselves out is all too often strange and incomprehensible to us. It is not simple to detect God's way in the course of history. All too often it is only with the benefit of hindsight that we may claim to have detected his acts. However, in spite of the fact that the prophet does not comprehend God's actions, he does not lose faith. He still appeals to the God he knows, the holy God from all eternity who cannot be indifferent to injustice. It is also significant that the kind of relationship the prophet has with this very God allows him to question his actions in an open and frank way.

iv. YHWH's second response (2:2–20)
a. To live by faith even in times of adversity (2:2–5)
Context

Habakkuk 2:2 is the start of a new unit. In view of the dialogue between Habakkuk and YHWH, this verse states that YHWH will now answer Habakkuk after Habakkuk's second complaint (1:12–17) which followed YHWH's initial response to the prophet (1:5–11). In the superscription of the book it was said that Habakkuk 'saw' a message or proclamation.

Comment

2. Here in verse 2 the prophet is told to *Write down* the vision that will be revealed to him. No indication is given of the time lapse between Habakkuk's second complaint and the answer now given by YHWH to the prophet. It is not possible to manipulate YHWH into giving an answer; suddenly YHWH's response comes. It is YHWH who commands his prophet to write the vision. The command further specifies that the vision should be made *plain on tablets*. The word used for *tablets* is the same one used for the stone tablets Moses used

(Exod. 32:15–16; 34:1, 4, 28–29; Nogalski 2011: 668). Elsewhere in the Old Testament, especially in the prophetic literature, there are commands to write down visions of prophecies received (Isa. 8:1–4; 30:8; Jer. 36:2, 32). In the second half of the verse the tablets are referred to in the singular (*it*). We can envisage the tablet(s) as a kind of huge banner or billboard that is easy to read by anyone who walks by. The text does not provide us with any information as to whether the tablets were made of stone or wood.

The extent of the vision is a bone of contention in the interpretation of this verse. Does the vision refer to the entire book, only Habakkuk 2, the woe oracles of 2:6–20 or only 2:4 (Dietrich 2016: 126)? If we imagine the tablet referred to as a kind of banner, then we should think of only 2:4 as the content of the vision made known to the prophet.

The second part of this verse is also problematic. How should we understand 'the one who runs' (according to a literal reading of the Hebrew text), and does this person call out or read the tablet? One way of interpreting the phrase is to understand it as 'so that the one reading it will run', implying that the message will be of such a nature that it will make readers run in terror (Haak 1992: 56). Another possibility is to take 'running' as a metaphor for 'living one's life, lifestyle, fulfilling an assigned task' (Bratcher 1984: 120). Roberts (1991: 109–110) detected an intentional double meaning in the phrase. On the one hand, the phrase meant 'Write the vision legibly on the tablets so that the one reading from it can read quickly'. At the same time there was a deeper meaning: 'Write the vision on the tablets and make its import plain so that the one reading can take refuge in it.' The solution of Robertson (1990: 170) is to understand that 'Habakkuk must inscribe his vision plainly so that he who proclaims it may run'. The idea is, then, that once the vision has been made public, the message must be proclaimed so that it may become known. This is also the line of interpretation followed by Dietrich (2016: 112–113) and Floyd (2000: 473). Another possibility is to understand the phrase as simply meaning that one should be able to read the vision with ease, with 'the eye running over the letters' (Bruce 1999: 859; Tuell 2016: 78), and that is the interpretation adopted here. Interpreting the phrase this way coheres well with the first part of the verse where the vision is to be written plainly on the tablet. One should also keep in mind that not many people were able to read or write, and therefore what was written had to be easy to read for everyone who had mastered the art.

3. Verse 3 is an encouragement to hold on to the promise of a vision yet to be revealed. The vision that is meant for this very moment in history will be revealed only at the appropriate determined time, and only YHWH will decide when that time will be. What is more, the vision will be a reliable one that can be trusted to take place. The future will confirm its trustworthiness. If, in the experience of the prophet and/or his listeners, it takes some time to come, the admonition is to hold on, for the vision will most certainly come and without any unnecessary delay. Even though the prophet has already waited for a considerable period of time for YHWH to intervene but without any action from his side, in addition to the time that has elapsed during this intense dialogue between the prophet and YHWH, he is told to wait a bit longer for YHWH to act. The vision will be YHWH's answer to the complaint of the prophet. To a certain extent, this verse is part of the answer to Habakkuk's complaint. The problem is not YHWH's inability to notice the destruction and injustice in society; the problem is the lack of patience on the part of the prophet. YHWH will reveal a vision of what is to happen in the future but at a time according to his plans.

4. Habakkuk 2:4 is a well-known text within the Christian (especially the Reformed) tradition, due to the interpretation given by the apostle Paul in Romans 1:16–17 and Galatians 3:11, as well as that given in Hebrews 10:37–38. It is also a controversial verse in Habakkuk because of the difficulties that arise in translating and interpreting it. Furthermore, this verse represents a definite turning point in the book as a whole as it contains the answer to Habakkuk's complaints.

The verse commences with a call to look or *See*. It has already been noticed that 'seeing' is an important marker in the book. Habakkuk looks at the injustice (1:3); YHWH responds with a call to look and see a wider horizon – the nations beyond the borders of Judah (1:5); and while YHWH's eyes are too pure to see evil (1:13), the prophet will be on the lookout and see (2:1) what YHWH's answer will be to his second complaint. Now, at verse 4, when YHWH's answer will be made known, the call is again to 'see'.

One way of starting to interpret the text is to note that a contrast is drawn between the *puffed up* and the *righteous* (Baker 1988: 60; Bruce 1999: 860; Nogalski 2011: 214). The ones described as *puffed up* are *not upright*. *Puffed up* may also be translated as 'the proud' (Robertson 1990: 174; Bruce 1999: 858) or 'swollen' (Haak 1992: 57); 'the presumptuous' (Dietrich 2016: 109); or 'the fainthearted' (Roberts 1991: 105). The people described here might best be understood as the Babylonians, but also those Habakkuk complained about initially, namely the people within Judah who are responsible for the destruction, violence, strife and conflict that has resulted in the Torah being paralysed and justice perverted. The 'puffed up' or 'the presumptuous' are not *upright* (meaning straight or level) and therefore they will not prevail. Despite all the power they now have, crushing other people, they eventually will perish. To be 'puffed up' or arrogant is, then, a summary of all that has been said about the behaviour of the coming threat of the Babylonians.

In stark contrast to the eventual fate of the proud or arrogant Babylonians, the way of the *righteous* is described. The concept of righteousness is first and foremost a term denoting relationship. In the case of the people of God the term has to do with the relationship between God and his people, but also, and equally importantly, the relationship between members of the covenant people. It was von Rad (1975: 370) who stated that 'There is absolutely no concept in the Old Testament with so central a significance for all the relationships of human life as that of righteousness'. Different relationships make different demands. Righteousness as a concept describing a relationship will look different in a marriage from righteousness in other family relationships or in one's business relationships. The righteous person is the one who lives up to the standards a particular relationship demands. In terms of the righteous person's relationship with God, he or she must live according to the stipulations of the covenant. To put it in a nutshell, one's relationship with God demands loyalty (love) to him, and one's relationship with one's fellow human beings demands the kind of behaviour that will be to the benefit of others and/or to society at large, which boils down to love for one's neighbour. The righteous are here encouraged to keep on practising this basic way of living: to live their lives in a close relationship with YHWH, the covenant God, and in a close relationship with their fellow human beings. Living this way will counter the violence and destruction, the strife and conflict, so that justice may be restored when people take the demands of the Torah seriously once again. The Torah, after all, has to do with regulating human relationships in order to live life in a peaceful and harmonious way. This positive way of depicting the righteous is in stark contrast to the descriptions in the previous units of the suffering the righteous have to endure.

The righteous will live through their steadfastness. What does steadfastness, or *faithfulness*, mean in this verse? The noun is derived from a verb that may be rendered 'to be reliable' or 'stable', hence the translations 'steadfastness', 'faithfulness' or 'trustworthiness'. One may also think of 'fidelity' or 'reliability' as possible renderings. The righteous should keep being steadfast and faithful, trusting God in these extremely trying times. The righteous will overcome the current period because they have kept the faith by remaining faithful to God. They will live because of the tenacity of their faithfulness to God. Righteous people stay committed to the trust they have in God even in dire circumstances. The righteous will live by and through faith in him. To be faithful has the connotation of being faithful to God and therefore of trusting him, come what may.

5. Surprisingly, verse 5 does not elaborate on the fate of the righteous but rather on that of the oppressor. The opening words ('moreover' or *indeed*) suggest a continuation of what was said in the previous verse. While the righteous must live steadfastly, the wicked will continue in their ways. Just as *wine* is treacherous, so also are the wicked Babylonian forces. Precisely because of that, however, they will not succeed. There is a glimmer of hope: the Babylonians will end up being betrayed by their own greed for more and more power. This terrible military force of the Babylonians is compared to *the grave*, or Sheol, the inescapable place where all people will end up, and to *death* itself. Just as death has an insatiable appetite that can never be satisfied, so the Babylonians have an insatiable appetite to subject nations under their control. The image of the Babylonians opening their throats to devour people recalls the earlier image in 1:13 where the wicked swallow up *those more righteous than themselves*. Verse 5 serves as a transition to the series of woe oracles in the next unit (2:6–20).

Meaning

It is a strange answer given to Habakkuk. The vision in no way explains or justifies God's actions through the Babylonian forces. It does not provide the prophet or the listeners to or readers of his prophecy with any insight into God's way of directing world affairs. Nor does God defend his actions to the prophet. However, neither Habakkuk nor the people have the ability to grasp how God governs world affairs; it is therefore of no use to reveal it to them. The 'why' questions of Habakkuk are not answered in a simple and direct way. Instead, the people of Judah are encouraged to remain faithful to YHWH by putting their trust in him. It is by doing so that they will live and eventually overcome their current hardship. That is what they need to know. The issue at stake is not how God governs world affairs; it is how believers react in difficult times.

b. The woe oracles (2:6–20)
Context

This unit is clearly marked as a series of five so-called 'woe oracles' (vv. 6b–8, 9–11, 12–14, 15–17, 18–19). However, it should also be noted that the woe oracles are not entirely disconnected from the previous unit. The pronouns found in the first line of verse 6 refer to the nations and peoples mentioned at the end of verse 5. The heading at the beginning of chapter 3 introduces a completely new unit, distinguishing it from the woe oracles only to be found in 2:6–20.

Comment

6–8. The thrust of the first part of verse 6 states that the people described in the previous units will eventually be punished. The words used (*taunt, ridicule, scorn*) make one think of wisdom literature. In Proverbs 1:6 the same verb here translated as 'taunt' is rendered as 'proverbs'. By making use of terms usually at home in a wisdom context, the first part of verse 6 gains a generalized meaning. That the evil people will be punished is not only true in the case of the Babylonians, but it is a general truth applicable to all oppressive forces. By making use of a wisdom saying, or a parable mixed with satire and figurative speech, this statement is made in a veiled way so that not everyone, and especially not the oppressive force, will understand its meaning. It suggests that it requires interpretation to gain an understanding of the content of the woe oracles that will follow. There is probably also a degree of mockery suggested. The mighty political force is mocked even before its inevitable downfall. In this way the present hardship the people have to endure will be made a little easier to bear. 'Absolute monarchs and vain tyrants tend to react with extreme petulance when they reap derision and mockery instead of respect and applause. There is hardly a more potent weapon against dictators than a joke' (Dietrich 2016: 145).

It is in verses 6b–8 that the first woe oracle is found. Woe oracles are found elsewhere in the Latter Prophets as well (Isa. 5:8–23; 10:1; 28:1; 29:15; 30:1; 31:1; 33:1; Amos 5:18; 6:1, 4). Originally the expression *Woe* was probably used in a funeral setting where the deceased was mourned. When the prophets then made use of the expression, it would have attracted the attention of listeners. Woe oracles are prophecies of judgment and doom directed at foreign rulers and nations as well as at the people of Israel. With the use of the *Woe* at the beginning of each of the five prophecies, the prophet in effect announces the death penalty upon the evil foreign people.

The first offence committed is stated clearly: they 'heap up what is not [their] own' (NRSV), which simply means that they have acquired in an unjust way possessions that did not belong to them. Once again, the offenders are not only the foreign power of Babylonia, but also the rich and arrogant people in Judah who *pile up stolen goods* that originally belonged to their fellow Judeans. The second offence was to take goods 'in pledge' (NRSV; NIV *by extortion*). The practice behind this offence was to make loans to the poor and vulnerable, with interest to be paid. In order to obtain a loan, a person needed to put down a deposit in the form of an item of value. This item was never returned to the borrower, who most probably was not in a position to repay the loan. The interesting turn in this woe oracle is that the one who is seen as providing

loans in an unjust way is then actually portrayed as a borrower
(v. 7). What was acquired in an unjust way was never intended to be
the property of the oppressor. What the Babylonians acquired by
their brutal seizing of power and subjecting of nations is seen as a
loan, and a loan has to be paid back sometime. What will happen
is that those who think of themselves as creditors, subjecting
people by demanding interest on loans that cannot be repaid, will
become the debtors; and, all of a sudden, those who are the debtors
will become the *creditors* and will claim back what has been taken
from them. These creditors will now be in a position of power, so
much so that the former creditors will be their victims (*their prey*).
In this way justice will be restored. The Torah had been paralysed
(1:4) by the abuse of the stipulations on lending practices in Deuteronomy 24, but that will be rectified and the justice that had been
perverted will be restored. What the oppressors did will now be
done to them. They were the ones who *plundered many nations*, but
now they themselves will be plundered. The reason for this reversal
of fortunes is summarized in the last two lines of verse 8: it is all
because of their shedding of human blood and the violence they
had done to the *lands* and *cities*. Robertson (1990: 190) speaks of
reciprocal judgment being exercised here.

   9–11. The second woe oracle continues to describe the inevitable downfall of the wicked. *Unjust gain* has been acquired in a
greedy way. The same verb (*builds*) is also found in Proverbs 15:27,
where it is used in the context of taking bribes. While those who
engage in unjust transactions bring trouble on their families, the
one who hates bribes will live. Once again it seems that Habakkuk
not only was aware of wisdom traditions but that he actively made
use of them to bring his message home. There is a nice play on
words in verse 9: 'evil gain' (NRSV) is used to keep them safe, but
that in itself is an evil practice. This evil gain will bring about
disaster even though it was intended to provide security against
possible invaders (Bratcher 1984: 181). The safe *nest* (Num. 24:21;
Job 39:27–28; Obad. 4) built *on high* (a metaphor for security) is not
safe! Possessions gained in this way do not make the wicked feel
really safe, and therefore there is a constant need for security.

   Instead of security, they have 'devised shame for [their] house'
(NRSV). Just as they took the lives of *many peoples*, their *life* will be

forfeited. So, by committing the evil verse 9 speaks of, and by killing many people, they have put their own lives in danger. In a strange and surprising way, the stolen materials, like the *stones* and the plaster or *beams* of the house, are personified. The normally silent stones and woodwork now *cry out* against the evil and unjust behaviour of an oppressive force. The strong house built for safety is on the brink of destruction and will in due time collapse completely.

12–14. The third woe oracle continues to denounce the efforts made by political powers to build their empires by means of bloodshed and injustice. The *city* and *town* mentioned in verse 12 refer to more than simply a city; they more probably refer to the building of the empire at large, although empires are known for their building projects as well. The point made is that an empire has been built through *bloodshed* and oppressive *injustice*. This is quite the opposite of what is stated in Proverbs 24:3, where the same verbs are used:

> By wisdom a house is built,
>> and through understanding it is established.

Whereas in the previous woe oracle the metaphor of a house was used, the metaphor is now expanded to the broader category of a city or town. The formulation of this woe reminds one of Micah 3:10:

> who build Zion with bloodshed,
>> and Jerusalem with wickedness.

Although this woe oracle is directed at the Babylonian Empire, the almost verbatim quote from Micah allows for an interpretation directed at the situation in Judah as well.

The sad fact is that, despite so much effort put into building enterprises by means of forced labour, which has resulted in the deaths of many, it will not last. What they have built will be consumed by *fire*, so those building the city will have done so in vain because it will come to *nothing* (v. 13). Because the empire in question was built through bloodshed and injustice, these building projects have been an exercise in futility. This futility becomes even more apparent when one keeps in mind that a city could burn down within a few hours, while building it represented years of hard work.

While nothing has been said of God's activity in the first two woe oracles, this third woe makes clear theological statements. Verse 13 states that it is not God's intention that people should build a city through forced labour, only for that city to be consumed by fire. Nations are not supposed to toil to the point of utter exhaustion *for nothing*. God is named as the LORD *Almighty* or 'YHWH of hosts'. To refer to God as 'YHWH of hosts' is to remind the people that God is indeed the master of the universe and the ultimate ruler, over and above all earthly rulers and kings, however mighty they may seem to be. The oracle concludes with a powerful positive statement about God: *the earth will be filled with the knowledge of the glory of* YHWH. Verse 14 is an almost verbatim quote from Isaiah 11:9. The same message once proclaimed in the Isaianic prophecy against the background of the mighty Assyrian Empire can now be repeated again. Just as the Assyrian Empire came to an end, so too will the Babylonian Empire. YHWH will intervene to deliver his people just as he did during the time of the Assyrian rulership. YHWH is not unaware or inactive, as was suggested by Habakkuk; on the contrary, he is YHWH, the God of hosts, ruler of all rulers.

15–17. In this fourth oracle another terrible practice of Babylon is denounced. What the Babylonians did was to let their neighbours drink wine to the point where they got *drunk*. This provided the Babylonians with an opportunity to view their neighbours in their *naked* state. The consequence was shame and humiliation for their opponents, stripping them of human dignity and honour, especially in the Ancient Near Eastern context of Old Testament times. Although the idea of seeing another human being's naked-ness has sexual connotations, we as the readers of the text are not given any more detail. It is therefore not possible to conclude with certainty that sexual or homosexual acts are implied here. It is known that prisoners of war were sometimes led away naked (Roberts 1991: 124), as Isaiah 20:4 and 2 Chronicles 28:15 indicate.

There are other places in the Old Testament/Hebrew Bible where becoming drunk on wine and uncovering a man's nakedness is reported in a negative sense. In Genesis 9 it is told how Noah planted a vineyard, drank some of its wine and then became drunk. One of Noah's son's, Ham, saw his father's nakedness. Lot's daughters devised a plan to get their father drunk so that they might get pregnant, and both daughters conceived and gave birth to Moab and Ammon (Gen. 19:30–38). In 2 Samuel 11:13 we read about David making his officer Uriah drunk. This happened in the context of the story of David and Bathsheba, the wife of Uriah. She became pregnant after David, having watched her while she was bathing, summoned her to his palace. David then arranged to have Uriah placed at the forefront of a battle, where he was killed. It is noteworthy that in all these cases, drunkenness and sexual violation go together (Dietrich 2016: 148).

There will, however, be a dramatic turn of events. Instead of the Babylonians handing a cup to other nations, YHWH will hand the Babylonians a cup for them to drink. It is explicitly said that they will have to drink the cup coming from the *right hand* of God (v. 16). The way they have treated others will now be the way God treats them. To drink from the cup from God denotes judgment (Janzen 1982: 408; Szeles 1987: 41) upon evil and wicked political powers – and this is also found in other parts of the Old Testament (Isa. 51:17–22; Jer. 25:15–28; 49:12; Ezek. 23:30–35). Just as others have been humiliated by having their nakedness exposed, so the oppressor will likewise now be put to shame. The glory of being victorious will turn into contempt and shame.

The woe oracle concludes with reiterating once again the reason for the judgment and punishment awaiting the Babylonians. It is because of the *human blood* they have shed and the destruction of *lands and cities*. The second half of verse 17 repeats almost verbatim the words found in verse 8. The interesting twist in verse 17 is the mention of *Lebanon*. Lebanon also had to suffer the violence of the Babylonians, and the *destruction of animals* terrified them. This may be a reference to Nebuchadnezzar's building projects in which he made use of the forests of Lebanon (Rudolph 1975: 228). What is interesting is that God not only cares for human beings suffering from the violence of a foreign power, but he also cares for the trees of Lebanon as well as the animals roaming the forests of Lebanon.

What is probably hinted at is the slaughtering of wild animals to feed the army of the Babylonians. God is not only God for his people; he is the universal Creator God who cares for his creation. We live in an age of worldwide concern about the condition of our planet, and especially about our responsibility in allowing the planet to degenerate to the condition it is in. This verse reveals God's concern for his creation. Human exploitation of the earth is an offence against nature, but, more importantly, it is a sin committed against, and deserving to be punished by, God, the creator of heaven and earth.

18–20. It is at once clear that the last oracle differs from the previous ones. In this case the *Woe* appears in the second half of the unit and not at the beginning, as in the previous woe oracles. A second difference concerns the theme of the oracle. In the previous oracles the theme was the violence and injustice the Babylonian forces had inflicted upon the people and upon other neighbouring peoples as well. Third, unlike the preceding oracles, there is no proclamation of judgment to be found here. Fourth, this last oracle is rather brief when compared with the other four oracles. In spite of all these differences, however, there are no compelling reasons to view these verses as a later insertion that is not properly in place here.

In this last oracle the theme is the futility of worshipping idols. Has the author/redactor made this last oracle different in order to bring the series of woe oracles to a climax? Is the point of this last oracle that ultimately it is all about who you worship? Who (or rather, what) you worship will determine the ethical and moral decisions you make.

What profit can there be in worshipping an *idol*? An idol is a *carved* or molten image created by the very one who now worships it. It is absurd to put your trust in and worship something that you yourself have created. If idols are man-made, it is self-evident that they cannot be real gods. If, then, idols are nothing more than carved or molten images, what people claim they are saying must be nothing more than lies. Idols made from *wood, stone* or metal are just that, wood, stone or metal, and therefore they cannot speak – they are speechless nothings (Robertson 1990: 208). Psalm 115 echoes the same message:

But their idols are silver and gold,
    made by human hands.
They have mouths, but cannot speak,
    eyes, but cannot see.
They have ears, but cannot hear,
    noses, but cannot smell.
They have hands, but cannot feel,
    feet, but cannot walk,
        nor can they utter a sound with their throats.
(Ps. 115:4–7)

It is a worthless exercise to call upon these man-made objects of worship. To call upon a piece of wood to *Wake up!* or a stone to rise is futile – it will not happen. Therefore, a woe is pronounced on those who do so. Even if an idol is decorated with *gold and silver* it remains nothing but a lifeless entity as it has *no breath* or spirit in it. The famous incident of Elijah and the priests of Baal on Mount Carmel (1 Kgs 18) comes to mind: the priests shouted louder and louder to Baal, but to no effect; and then Elijah taunted them: 'Surely he is a god!... Maybe he is sleeping and must be awakened' (1 Kgs 18:27). To expect *guidance* or teaching from a lifeless object, even if it is decorated with gold or silver, is to expect the impossible: it just will not happen. The actions of a foreign power are in the end driven by deeper religious convictions. Within the span of a few cryptic sentences Habakkuk makes a polemical mockery of powerless idols worshipped as gods by the Babylonians. Such mockery of idols worshipped as gods by other nations is found elsewhere in the Old Testament/Hebrew Bible as well (Pss 115:8; 135:18; Isa. 40:19; 42:17; 44:9–14; 46:1–2; Jer. 10:5; 11:12; 16:19; Hos. 8:4; 13:2). Moreover, idolatry is also forbidden in the Torah (Exod. 20:3–6; Deut. 4:28; 28:36, 64).

The series of woe oracles comes to an end with a solemn call to be silent in the presence of YHWH who resides in his temple. In contrast to the man-made nonentities worshipped as gods is YHWH, present in his *holy temple*. In the previous verses the people were calling upon their so-called gods to wake up and arise. Now the people are called upon to *be silent* in the presence of YHWH as he is the one who has revealed his plan by speaking to the prophet. The call to be silent in

the presence of YHWH is also found elsewhere in the prophetic literature (Amos 6:10; 8:3; Zeph. 1:7; Zech. 2:13). As YHWH is the one and
only true God, it is fitting that the whole world be silent in his
presence. Once more, it is reiterated that YHWH is more than a local
god; he is indeed the Lord of all nations (*all the earth*) (Snyman 2003:
430). It is not certain whether the heavenly abode or the temple in
Jerusalem is meant here. Perhaps a too sharp contrast should not be
made between the two possibilities, as Psalm 11:4 says that YHWH is
in his holy temple while his throne is in heaven (Bruce 1999: 876).
Whatever the case may be, the temple is seen as the dwelling place
of YHWH. He is thus neither absent nor inactive. When there is a call
to be silent in the presence of God it signals his imminent
intervention that will certainly take place (Bratcher 1984: 206).

Verse 20 serves as a transition between the woe oracles and the
prayer of Habakkuk in the next chapter.

Meaning
In five woe oracles foreign nations who are victors and oppressors
are ridiculed for their misdeeds. It is especially their treatment of
the people of other nations that has come under the judgment of
the prophet. They have acquired wealth in ways that cannot be
justified. They have committed injustices against other people by
destroying property and killing them. Even more than that, they
have put their trust in worthless and lifeless gods. The so-called
'gods' are unmasked as nothing but idols. In a reversal of fortunes
YHWH will restore justice. Eventually the nations who know no
limit to their power will have to drink the cup from YHWH's right
hand, indicating judgment and the restoration of justice. The call
to be silent in the presence of YHWH is therefore apt because those
who remain faithful may expect his intervention. Sometimes
believers under oppression can do little more than hold on to
God's promises. It is the firm belief that he will intervene that
keeps them going during times of suffering beyond comprehension.

C. The prayer-cum-psalm of the prophet Habakkuk (3:1–19)

Context
This unit displays the following macro-structure:

3:1a Superscription
A   3:1b Musical direction
B   3:2 The prophet calls upon YHWH
C   3:3–7 The coming of YHWH
C' 3:8–15 God is a warrior
B' 3:16 The prophet reacts
D   3:17–19a The prophet's confession of faith
A' 3:19b Musical direction

The chapter has a clear concentric structure, with the start and end of the unit providing the reader with a musical direction. The C parts of the unit, focusing on the majesty and power of YHWH, are framed by a call upon YHWH by the prophet and the prophet's reaction to the theophany described in 3:3–15. The D part (3:17–19a) does not follow the concentric structure and therefore attracts the attention of the reader.

Comment
i. Superscription (3:1)
1. Verse 1 is the superscription to the rest of the book and a clear marker that it represents a new start to a separate unit. The verse begins by designating it as a *prayer* – a not-unfamiliar heading found in the book of Psalms (17:1; 86:1; 90:1; 102:1; 142:1). The proper noun *Habakkuk* is mentioned again, together with his designation as a *prophet*, as in Habakkuk 1:1. Now that Habakkuk has seen the vision (1:1), this second part of the book is his response to it by way of prayer. The dialogical structure characteristic of the first part of the book is maintained in the second part.

The superscription is then followed by a musical direction as is found in many psalms. The term *shigionoth* remains a mystery and is therefore best left untranslated, but it is also found in its singular form in the heading of Psalm 7. The closing words of the prayer in verse 19b, *For the director of music. On my stringed instruments*, together with the term *Selah* which in the Hebrew is found no less than three times (vv. 3, 9, 13; cf. NIV margin) in this prayer, confirm its psalm-like style. Habakkuk 3 is thus presented as a prayer in the form of a psalm or, conversely, as a psalm in the form of a prayer. The musical directions at the beginning and end of the prayer/psalm

form a nice *inclusio* bracketing chapter 3 as a distinctive part of the
book.

ii. The prophet calls upon YHWH (3:2)

2. Verse 2 is the start of the prayer and calls upon YHWH. The
prophet has heard the reports about him and his *deeds* have evoked
fear in the prophet. The change in the tone of his prayer compared
to the accusations he levelled against YHWH in the first part of
the book is significant. Instead of questioning God, the prophet
now humbles himself in God's presence (2:20) and *stand[s] in awe*
before his *deeds*. God's *deeds* refers to what he has done in the past,
namely his acts of deliverance in the history of his people. The plea
of the prophet is that such wonderful acts may be revived in the
present time. The future, in other words, is revealed in the past:
what God has done in the past is the model for what believers may
ask and expect of him in the future. Earlier the prophet had asked
for YHWH to execute and restore justice; now he pleads for *mercy*
in the midst of God's *wrath*. The past is a witness to YHWH's glorious and awe-inspiring mighty acts of deliverance, the present is a
time of turmoil and distress, but the future will bring deliverance
again.

This is the kind of situation many believers of all times can
recognize. They often find themselves in a similar predicament as
the prophet. There is sometimes a dissonance between God's acts
in the past and the present trying circumstances. There is also
sometimes a dissonance between God's promises of future deliverance and the current situation. This tension is resolved by a plea for
mercy. The word translated *mercy* can also be rendered 'compassion',
'pity' or 'covenant faithfulness' (Bratcher 1984: 241).

iii. The coming of YHWH (3:3–7)

3–7. In this unit YHWH's coming is described. The first word in
verse 3 is *God* ('*ĕlôah* in Hebrew), a seldom-used term for God where
one would rather expect the more familiar YHWH or '*ĕlōhîm*. The
same term is used in 1:11, but in that verse the term 'god' refers to
the god in which the oppressor finds his strength. Here in 3:3 the
term is used to indicate that God, the God of Israel, will come. The
verse states that God comes from *Teman* and *Mount Paran*. There is

general consensus that these geographical indications refer to a region south of Israel in the southern part of Edom. This brings to mind the deliverance of Israel from the bondage of Egypt. God is portrayed as the God who once victoriously delivered his people from Egypt to lead them to the Promised Land (Deut. 33:2; Judg. 5:4–5; Ps. 68:7–9). *Teman* and *Mount Paran* (together with *Cushan* and *Midian* mentioned in v. 7) are also associated with Sinai (van der Woude 1978: 67; Rudolph 1975: 243; Snyman 2003: 431). Sinai was the place where God revealed himself in a mighty theophany as the covenant God, where he entered into a covenant with his people and where he gave them the Torah. Not only is God the God of deliverance, but he is also the God of the covenant. His *glory* covers the whole of the universe as the *heavens* are covered by his *glory* and the *earth* is full of his *praise*. It is possible that *glory* and *praise* refer to meteorological phenomena similar to those in the exodus tradition (Roberts 1991: 152). God is also described as the *Holy One*, emphasizing his otherness and that he will come to judge the unjust in the world (Szeles 1987: 47). Within the span of a few words several major traditions of Israel are thus brought to mind: the exodus from Egypt, the Sinai event, consisting of a theophany and the covenant, and the entry into the land. As God came in the past to deliver his people, so he will come to deliver his people again. Halfway through verse 3 is found the word *Selah*, a term that apart from Habakkuk is found only in the Psalms. Its meaning remains a mystery but usually it is assumed to be a kind of musical term. Verse 4 continues to describe the majesty of God. His brightness can be compared to the *sunrise*. The weapons he uses are like light (lightning?) that flashes from his hand. Yet, at the same time, not all his might is revealed; his mighty strength is *hidden*. The full revelation of God's power is too much for mortal human beings; it is more than they can imagine it to be.

Unique to the book of Habakkuk, God in his coming is accompanied by two seemingly powerful demonic figures, *plague* (*deber*) which goes in front of him and *pestilence* (*rešep*) which follows behind. These may be understood as personifications of destruction but may also refer to foreign deities. Nogalski (2011: 683–684) as well as Dietrich (2016: 168) have noted that, while *deber* is less well attested, *rešep* is known as a warrior god from the Ebla texts as

well as in Ugarit, Phoenicia and Canaan. Figures recognized as
deities in other cultures are here shown as mere assistants and
servants of YHWH, accompanying him on his triumphant journey
as the ultimate ruler of the earth. The role these two figures will
play is clear: they will act as instruments in the hands of YHWH to
punish the enemies.

Both the earth and its inhabitants are affected by YHWH's coming.
YHWH stands and measures (NIV *shook*) the earth – a vivid indication
of his majesty and greatness. *Mountains* and *hills*, symbols of eternity,
are shattered and *nations tremble*. The earth is at his disposal and he
can do with it whatever he wants. The nations, as the inhabitants
of the earth, can only tremble when he appears. The whole of creation is aware of YHWH's awesome coming and there is no use
trying to resist him. Both nature and humanity are subdued before
him, the all-powerful God. Just as God long ago liberated his
people from oppression, so he will do again, thereby walking 'along
his ancient pathways' (NRSV). The Bedouins in the land of *Midian*
will experience the effect of God's coming first as God will advance
from the south where they have their *tents*.

iv. God is a warrior (3:8–15)

This unit has quite an interesting structure:

    A The sea and rivers as mighty powers (v. 8)
    B YHWH's weapons: bow and arrows and a spear (v. 9a)
    C The effect God's appearance has on nature (vv. 9b–11)
    D God's anger as viewed by the earth and the nations (v. 12)
    C' The effect of God's appearance both on his people and
       on the enemy (v. 13)
    B' YHWH's weapons: spears (v. 14)
    A' The sea and the deep waters in history (v. 15)

Verses 8–15 thus also display a concentric structure. Verse 12 (part
D) forms the centre of this unit and serves as a transition from
God's mighty power as revealed in nature to his power revealed to
people. The first part of verse 12 speaks of YHWH's acts in nature
while the second part speaks of his acts among the nations. God's
anger mentioned in verse 8 is mentioned again in verse 12.

8–9a. Verse 8 introduces a new unit in this chapter. YHWH is addressed by a vocative, with the prophet calling upon him. In the previous unit (3:3–7) God was described in third-person singular forms, but in this unit there is a change to second-person singular forms. Furthermore, in verses 3–7 God was referred to as *'ĕlôah*, while in this unit 'YHWH' is used to address him.

In verse 8 a rhetorical question is posed to YHWH. Is his anger, *wrath* and *rage* directed towards the rivers and the sea? The mention of rivers and sea brings to mind conflicts with the powers of chaos in Semitic mythology. One could think here of Marduk's victory over Tiamat (the deep sea) or the victory of Baal over Yam (the sea) (Bruce 1999: 886). God acting against the rivers and sea may also remind the people of the deliverance from Egypt when the Red Sea was parted so that Israel could safely escape from the Egyptian army, which was destroyed by the sea (Exod. 13 – 14; van der Woude 1978: 69–71; Szeles 1987: 48, 54). Thus God proved to be victorious in the past, and his past victories will now be repeated when he acts against the Babylonians. YHWH is further portrayed as a warrior riding *horses* with *chariots*.

What is new to this unit is the mention of the anger of God. He is not aloof or inactive concerning world events, especially where his people are suffering injustice; on the contrary, he is moved to the point of anger and is therefore on his way to act. The rhetorical question asked is apt. God's anger is not directed against the rivers and the sea; it is directed at the nations responsible for the injustices and destruction his people have to suffer.

The first part of verse 9 confronts the interpreter with a multitude of problems. Robertson (1990: 233) noted that more than a hundred different explanations have been offered. The difficulties presented by this verse are seen in the variety of translations offered in commentaries. Although verse 9a is a difficult text to interpret, the image of God as a warrior riding horses with a chariot is continued. God is presented as uncovering his *bow* to make use of a bow and arrow as his weapon. The chariot serves as a metaphor for clouds. The second line of the verse is even more difficult to understand. The idea seems to be that the arrows shot with the bow are 'sated' (NRSV), in the sense that they have found their targets.

9b–12. Various elements of creation (*earth, mountains, water, the deep, sun, moon*) dominate these verses. Creation reacts to the mighty appearance of God. In poetic language rivers are described as changing the surface of the earth by forming rifts, thereby creating the image of having *split* it. Mountains tremble, meaning that earthquakes occur. Water is both a blessing and a threat. The noise of rushing water coming in torrents, roaring, surging and sweeping by, can be terrifying, even more so when it is seen as a reaction to the manifestation of the power of YHWH (Snyman 2003: 431). The rushing of water may also be reminiscent of an invading army (Haak 1992: 96). It seems best to interpret the 'voice from the deep' (*the deep roared*) as the sound of the roaring waves of the sea: YHWH's appearance is likened to this sound. Even celestial bodies, the sun and moon, are affected by the light of YHWH's arrows flashing by. In short, the mighty powers of creation acknowledge the even greater power of YHWH. Verse 12 makes it clear that while the forces of nature acknowledge the mighty power of YHWH, his actions are not aimed at them but rather at *the nations*. In fact, verse 12 forms the transition from the reaction of the created order to the fearful appearance of YHWH, to his actions directed towards people.

13. In the original complaint of the prophet he cried out that YHWH did not save his people (1:2). Here in verse 13 the confirmation is given that YHWH will indeed come to save them. Significantly, the verb 'to save', or *deliver*, occurs twice in this verse. YHWH will come to save his people and his *anointed one*. How should *your anointed one* be interpreted? It was kings and high priests who were known to be anointed in Old Testament times. In verse 13 the *anointed one* does not refer to a priest-like figure, so that possibility can be ruled out. That leaves us with a king. Was Habakkuk thinking of one of the last Judean kings during the final years of Judah before the Babylonian exile? Probably not, because from the first complaint of the prophet (1:2–4) it seems that the destruction, violence, strife, conflict and perversion of justice were internal problems, with the king being the one who had the responsibility of ruling to the benefit of the people. It is improbable that the prophet thought of one of the last kings of Judah as an anointed one of YHWH. It seems best, therefore, to interpret *your anointed one* as part of a parallelism with *your people*, referring to the people of

God. They are regarded as YHWH's anointed one and therefore will be delivered from the ordeal they are now suffering.

While the people of God will be saved, the 'head of the wicked house' (NRSV) will be *crushed*. There is a degree of ambiguity in this second part of verse 13. Does the 'head of the wicked house' refer to the leader of the nation that oppresses the people of God? Or does the wording point to the leader together with his kingdom ('house') that will be defeated, including its buildings, exposing their 'foundation' up to its 'roof' (neck; NRSV)? Perhaps the ambiguity of the text should be appreciated in this case. It is possible, then, that both the leader and his kingdom, together with the buildings, will be defeated and thoroughly destroyed. Interestingly, the deliverance of the people is mentioned first, indicating that it is the deliverance of the people that is important and not the crushing of an enemy. God has to act against the oppressor of his people to save them.

14. The interpretation of verse 14 is hampered by textual uncertainties. The thrust of the argument is, however, clear. The oppressive enemy will be destroyed. Once again YHWH is the one who will act on behalf of his people, making use of a *spear* to defeat the enemy. Even though their warriors may try to *storm* against the people and *scatter* them, eager to *devour* the poor while they are *hiding*, the victory will belong to God.

15. Verse 15 returns to the same metaphors used in verse 8, but with a difference. In verse 8 it was said that YHWH rode out with horses to engage in a war with the oppressor. In verse 15 the war has been won as the sea has been *trampled*. Mention of the sea recalls God's decisive deliverance on behalf of his people at the Red Sea. As God once delivered his people from the bondage of Egypt, so he will deliver them again in similar fashion.

v. *The prophet reacts (3:16)*

16. Verse 16 marks a turning point in this last chapter. In 3:2 the prophet called upon YHWH, starting with the words *I have heard of your fame*. In verse 16 the same first-person singular form of the same verb is used: 'I have heard.' Verse 16 thus recalls the initial prayer of the prophet begun in verse 2, and in this way verses 2 and 16 serve as a nice frame to the main part of the chapter. YHWH is also no longer addressed as he was in the previous part; rather, an account is given of the prophet's own reaction to the vision of God's majestic power in verses 3–15. Verse 16 consists of two distinctive parts. On the one hand, the prophet is overwhelmed by what he has just experienced. On the other hand, in a sudden turn of emotion, he states that he will wait patiently for the day of calamity to come.

The prophet's reaction to this visionary experience of God's awesome power is described in physical terms. The prophet's body reacted to this mighty theophany physically: his *lips quivered*, he felt *decay* (a weakness; lit. rottenness) in his *bones*, and he found it difficult to walk as his legs felt numb and even paralysed. This kind of reaction is not unique to Habakkuk; 'although nowhere is it painted so intensely as it is here' (Dietrich 2016: 175), other prophets had similar experiences (Isa. 21:3–4; Jer. 4:19; Dan. 7:15; 8:27; 10:9).

In the end the prophet surrenders to YHWH's overwhelming power. His initial questioning of YHWH's ability to act against the injustices he observed gives way to humble submission. The fear the prophet has is combined with trust and faith in YHWH. Verse 16 conveys the sense of numinous dread (or *tremendum*) and at the same time fascination (or *fascinosum*) by which Habakkuk is drawn into an attitude of acceptance and commitment (Janzen 1982: 411). Habakkuk does what he was told to do in 2:3: 'wait for it'. He is convinced that God will intervene on a *day* he will decide upon. For the moment, Habakkuk is content with the assurance that a day of judgment will also come upon the people who are attacking them, even though it might not (and did not) happen during his lifetime. Eventually it happened when the Babylonian Empire was replaced by the Persian Empire, and Cyrus became the next world leader, in 539 BC.

vi. The prophet's confession of faith (3:17–19a)

17–19a. Verse 17 marks the beginning of the penultimate unit in chapter 3. The vocabulary used in these verses is unique to the book. Terminology at home in an agricultural environment occurs: *fig-tree, grapes* and *vines, olive crop, sheep* and *cattle*. What is also peculiar to these verses is that each line is internally paralleled in such a way that the first half of each line is balanced by a similar construction in the second half (vv. 17a=17b; 17c=17d; 17e=17f; 18a=18b; 19b=19c). Verse 17 is also structured to form a chiastic pattern: (A) the fig tree (B) shall not blossom (B') and no fruit (A') on the vines; (A) shall fail (B) the making of the olive (B') and the fields (A') shall not make food; (A) shall be cut off from the field (B) the flock (B') and no cattle (A') in the stalls (Robertson 1990: 244–245; Dietrich 2016: 176). Verse 19a breaks this pattern by having no balancing part and thus attracts attention as a focal point (Bratcher 1984: 276). Considering the macro-structure of the chapter as a whole, it is also striking that these verses do not fit in well with the concentric structure of the unit. This phenomenon also attracts attention to this part in particular.

Up to now the book has been interested in issues of justice, violence and destruction, first in Judean society (2:2–4) but then also in the arena of world history (1:5 – 2:19). How is it possible that a mere human being can have an insight into the way in which God exercises control of world affairs? Verses 17–19a turn to the small world of an everyday farmer in Judah trying to make a living on a smallholding of some kind. Notwithstanding the bigger picture of world history, making a living as a farmer who has to cope with crop failure is not easy. Life itself is at stake when the land does not yield any crops. The produce mentioned covers all the necessities to make a decent living in Old Testament times: fruit, olives for cooking, grapes and wine, grain to bake bread, clothing from sheepskins, milk and meat.

No indication is given in the text as to what the cause of the famine is. It is therefore futile to speculate whether it will be the result of the invading army or even the effect of YHWH's coming as described in verses 3–15. While believers must wait upon God to intervene in a decisive way sometime in the future, they have to make a living in the present in dire circumstances. Habakkuk does not present believers with a 'pie in the sky when you die' kind of theology. In the hard and pressing times of the present, believers should keep the faith, as was revealed to the prophet in 2:4. There is thus no need to view verses 17–19a as a secondary gloss to the unit.

Even in a situation where the prophet has had serious questions about YHWH and his apparent inability to intervene when justice is perverted; where the only answer he has received is to keep faith and believe that God will intervene at a time deemed appropriate; and where the ordinary farmer has to cope with a severe drought and famine, Habakkuk nevertheless rejoices in YHWH. YHWH is praised as the God of his salvation. The beginning of verse 18 starts with 'but as for me' to put the emphasis on the personal character of this remarkable confession of faith. The chapter, and for that matter the book, culminates, then, in a powerful confession of faith. Even when the necessities for making a living are no longer available, and when it is difficult if not impossible to detect God's control of world affairs, he still puts his trust in God. Earlier on in the book the prophet launched the accusation against God that he does not save (1:2). Right at the end of the book God is praised as *my Saviour* (3:18). Habakkuk is now convinced that as God once came to deliver his people, so he will come to deliver them again (3:13).

God is no longer perceived as aloof or inactive. Habakkuk now has an experience of God's presence in the midst of all the turmoil. God is his *strength*. To describe this experience of God Habakkuk uses a strong word that can also be rendered 'my army', perhaps in contrast to the coming Babylonian oppressor who is known to worship his military might as a god (1:11) (Roberts 1991: 158). In a telling metaphor the prophet likens himself to a *deer* or a hind walking dangerous routes along mountaintops, but he is kept safe and is even able to go on to the *heights*. Deer living in mountainous areas find their way in rocky and sometimes slippery places. Habakkuk, through his renewed trust and faith in God as his strength and Saviour, will also find his way through tough and trying times. It should also be noted that Habakkuk has come to this renewed trust and faith not because he has witnessed the precise outcome of the promises YHWH has made to him, but even though the restoration of justice is yet to come. In this sense Habakkuk is a living example of what it means to live by faith.

vii. A musical direction (3:19b)

19b. This chapter commences and comes to an end with a musical direction, creating an *inclusio* which binds the whole chapter together as a unit. The expression *For the director of music* or 'choir master' is found numerous times in the book of Psalms (Pss 4 – 6;

8 – 9; 11 – 14; 18 – 22; 31; 36; 39 – 42; 44 – 47; 49; 51 – 62; 64 – 70;
75 – 77; 80 – 81; 84 – 85; 88; 109; 139 – 140), and *On my* [or 'with']
stringed instruments at least five times (Ps. 4; 6; 54; 67; 76), but never
at the end of a psalm. It is possible that verse 19b was added later
to the unit, but that is impossible to determine beyond any doubt.
These directions point to the possibility that this psalm/prayer was
taken up in the believing community and was sung, perhaps by a
guild of temple singers (Bruce 1999: 896).

Meaning

In the end Habakkuk was a prophet who practised what he
preached. He had to proclaim faith in God in spite of his own
initial complaints, questions, misunderstanding and mistrust, and
he trusted God in a new way, even though his questions were not
answered in the way he expected them to be. At the end of the book
it becomes clear that God does not change – he is still the God
of justice, and in the end his justice will prevail. What did change
was the prophet's perception of God. He who dared to question
God was overwhelmed by the sheer majesty of God. As a result
of his changed perception of God, the book that began with a
complaint ends with a joyful hymn of trust. Habakkuk received
a quite unexpected answer to his questions, but this answer was
enough and his faith was strengthened.

Little wonder, then, that this remarkable confession of faith in
the midst of so much trial and tribulation has found its way to the
church in a hymn by William Cowper:

> Though vine nor fig tree neither
> Their wonted fruit should bear,
> Though all the field should wither,
> Nor flocks nor herds be there;
> Yet God the same abideth,
> His praise shall tune my voice,
> For, while in him confiding,
> I cannot but rejoice.[2]

---

2. William Cowper, 'Sometimes a Light Surprises'.

ZEPHANIAH

INTRODUCTION

The book of Zephaniah contributes a unique perspective on God, the people of God and the way in which God is active in creation, world affairs and the plight of his people. The book presents the reader with an interesting (and perplexing!) kaleidoscope of a universal outlook, including the whole of creation, the nations and a focus on the people of God. While judgment is pronounced on the other nations, there is at the same time the possibility of forgiveness and redemption. The same can be said of God's own people: they are also judged for their sins, but then there is the possibility of restoration.

1. Dating the book

In the very first verse of the book the reader is informed that Zephaniah's prophecy came *during the reign of Josiah son of Amon king of Judah.* Josiah's reign can be dated between the years 639 and 609 BC. In 2 Kings 22 – 23 (2 Chr. 34:1 – 35:19) a report is given on the reign of Josiah where he is hailed as one of the kings who 'did what was right in the eyes of the LORD and followed completely the ways of his father David, not turning aside to the right or to the left' (2 Kgs 22:2). His father, Amon, and grandfather, Manasseh, stand in stark contrast to Josiah. Amon had a brief reign of only two years and the verdict upon his reign is straightforward: 'He did evil in the eyes of the LORD, as his father Manasseh had done' (2 Kgs 21:20); his time is dealt with in only seven verses (2 Kgs 21:19–25). After Amon was assassinated, he was succeeded by Josiah, who was only eight years old. King Manasseh, Amon's predecessor, was an even worse king who reigned for no less than fifty-five years (2 Kgs 21:1–18).

When Josiah became king of Judah in 640/639 BC, the mighty Assyrian Empire was on the decline. The Assyrian ruler Ashurbanipal died around 630 BC and that resulted in a civil war within the Assyrian Empire. While the Assyrian Empire was in decline, however, the Babylonians were on the rise, increasingly becoming a force to be reckoned with. These international conditions left Josiah with a relatively free hand to carry out the reforms for which he is known. A weakened Assyria did not have the appetite or the capacity to keep a firm hand on the growing independence of Judah. The reforms Josiah began in 622 BC were initiated by the recovery of the Book of the Law by Hilkiah, the high priest. This book, identified as (at least part of) the book of Deuteronomy, was read to the king by Shaphan, the secretary at the temple. As a result, the king renewed the covenant and then cleansed the land of shrines, altars and high places dedicated to foreign gods. These reform initiatives did not all materialize at once; it is better to assume that they occurred over a period of time. Josiah was killed by Neco, king of Egypt, at Megiddo when he confronted the Egyptian king in battle (610/609 BC).

Zephaniah's prophecies fit in well within this time frame. Assyria and its capital Nineveh are targeted, together with other nations as well. It therefore seems safe to suppose a date prior to the fall of Nineveh in 612 BC. To pinpoint Zephaniah's prophecies to a closer date is problematic as there is little or no historical information given in the book itself. Did Zephaniah act before or after the reforms King Josiah initiated? If a date after the reforms of Josiah is preferred, it would seem strange that in 1:8 the royal household are addressed because of their custom of clothing themselves in foreign clothes. It would be odd that the people closely associated with the king should be guilty of the kind of sinful practices mentioned there. It is also hard to explain why the reforms of Josiah are not mentioned at all in the book, as the prophet would surely be positive about this initiative. A date closer to the reign of Josiah's predecessors and towards the beginning of his reign therefore seems more likely. In the light of the grave situation in which Manasseh and Amon left the country, total destruction awaited. Josiah became king at the age of eight but his reforms were begun only when he was twenty-six years old, in 622 BC. It might even be that Zephaniah's prophecies prompted Josiah to begin his reforms even before the discovery of the Book of the Law in the temple.

Taking all the arguments into consideration, Zephaniah was a contemporary of Nahum and Habakkuk as well as of the prophet Jeremiah. As with both Nahum and Habakkuk, nothing is known about Zephaniah the man. Even his genealogy, which goes back no less than four generations, tells us almost nothing about the prophet. The exegesis of verse 1 shows that it is unlikely that Zephaniah descended from the royal family, even though the mention of Hezekiah is probably a reference to the king. When reading the book, it becomes clear that Zephaniah had a grasp of the politics beyond the borders of Judah, as he mentions several cities and countries even as far away as Cush (roughly today's Ethiopia). Interestingly, Babylon is not mentioned, which might be another indicator of a date closer to the beginning of Josiah's reign. It is also noteworthy that he mainly addressed the elite of society, such as the royal officials, judges, prophets and priests, and paid no attention to the ordinary poor Israelite trying to make a living.

2. Literary issues

a. Literary genres used

Scholars agree that the 'book contains poetry on a very high level' and that it makes use of 'creative language that is unrivalled' (Dietrich 2016: 187). The book employs various literary genres, such as announcements of doom, announcements of salvation, hymns on the Day of YHWH, prophecies for other nations and the so-called woe oracle. The book is also rich in literary devices such as word-play, alliteration, rhyme, *inclusio*, chiasm and paranomasia (cf. the commentary).

b. Textual issues

Scholars agree that the text of Zephaniah is in a relatively good condition. Like all other books in the Old Testament there are text-critical problems, but there are no major issues. Some scholars (Ben Zvi 1991; Ufok Udoekpo 2010; Dietrich 2016) argue for a multi-layered book that evolved in different stages over a period of time. The current trend tends to look for cohesion, not only in the different units but also in the book as a whole. The conclusion Motyer (1998: 900) came to is that 'the book consists of carefully honed oracles accurately built into a coherent message'.

3. An outline of the theological message of Zephaniah

Zephaniah is a book that is thoroughly theological in nature. It starts with 'The word of YHWH' (1:1) and comes to a close with 'says YHWH' (3:20). In this way the book forms an *inclusio*, making it clear that it should be read as a word of YHWH literally from beginning to end. The theological message of the book may be summarized in three different portrayals of God.

a. YHWH *the God of creation*

The book commences with a powerful statement on YHWH who is about to destroy the earth. The God who is the God of creation announces his intention to destroy his creation. Everything will be swept away from the face of the earth: human beings, animals, birds and fish. God is about to undo creation. The phrase *from the face of the earth* found twice in 1:2–3 occurs no less than three times in the flood story recorded in Genesis (Gen. 6:7; 7:4; 8:8) (Redelinghuys 2017: 805). It seems clear that the announcement of doom upon the earth is informed by the flood story in Genesis. YHWH who once had the power to create also has the power to destroy creation, and the flood story is ample evidence that he exercised that power in the past. Although it will be *mankind* that will be destroyed from *the face of the earth* (1:3), the reason for this terrible judgment is the sins of Judah and Jerusalem (1:4).

b. YHWH *the God of judgment*

YHWH is also portrayed as the God of judgment. In line with the universal outlook that God is the God of creation, his judgment is directed towards both his own covenant people and the foreign nations. Judah is accused of idolatry, worshipping foreign gods and taking part in religious practices that are foreign to the way YHWH should be worshipped. Even more interesting is that the people are also accused of what we may call practical atheism. Judah has become indifferent to God. To Judah it seems that God is neither active nor passive. According to their observation, YHWH *will do nothing, either good or bad* (1:12). The prophet also speaks out against social injustices in society. To acquire wealth by making use of violence and deceit is simply not right in the eyes of the just God of the covenant. True religion is to worship YHWH alone and to practise justice towards one's fellow human beings.

Foreign nations are also addressed. Once again, the prophecies directed against foreign nations are in line with the portrayal of God as the universal God of creation. Gaza, Ashkelon, Ashdod, Ekron, the Kerethites, Moab, Ammon, Cush and Assyria are all addressed and their sins are pointed out. The verdict pronounced upon them is devastating: they will lose the land they occupy. The importance in Old Testament times of having land to cultivate, from which to make a living, can hardly be overstated. To lose land means to be cut off from the soil that provides for one's daily needs.

The verdict upon the people of God will be executed on the Day of YHWH – perhaps the most important theme in the book. The theme of the Day of YHWH is found only in the Latter Prophets in the Old Testament and is used, chronologically speaking, for the first time in Amos 5:18–20. Initially, the phrase was interpreted as positive for the people of God. The Day of YHWH will be a day of doom and judgment for the nations but of salvation for the people of God. Thus the Day of YHWH was perceived as a day to look forward to. The prophets turned this kind of interpretation in quite the opposite direction by insisting that the coming day will also mean judgment and disaster for the people of God.

Although the term 'Day of YHWH' occurs only in 1:7 and twice in 1:14, there are numerous other references to 'the day' (1:9–10, 18; 3:16). The Day of YHWH is the day when YHWH will be experienced not as the God who does *nothing, either good or bad* (1:12) but as the God who is active within the realm of his people and in fact the whole of creation.

c. YHWH *the God of salvation*
The announcement of judgment on the Day of YHWH is not the execution of judgment. Even when it seems that there is no other possibility left than utter destruction there is a glimmer of hope. The people are given yet another chance to repent. They are called to come together, seek YHWH in all humility and seek righteousness. Maybe the judgment will be averted. In a surprising announcement it is foreseen that once all the foreign gods have been destroyed YHWH *will be awesome to them* (2:11) and they will worship him instead of the worthless gods. In an equally astonishing statement it is foreseen that the lips of the foreign nations will be purified so that they may call upon the name of YHWH and *serve him shoulder to shoulder* (3:9). The last part of the book (3:14–20) contains some of the most moving declarations of love YHWH has made to his people.

In a strange and incomprehensible way, the announcements of judgment are counterbalanced by the promises of salvation, restoration and the love of God.

The universal perspective of the book is quite remarkable. It starts with a universal perspective on creation at large. Foreign nations are addressed and, as in the case of God's own people, judgment and salvation are announced to them. The coming Day of YHWH is also painted not as a local event but as a cosmic one in which *the whole earth* (1:18) will be consumed. When salvation is proclaimed, it likewise is not seen as a local event pertaining only to the people living in the land of Judah; YHWH will bestow honour and praise *among all the peoples of the earth* (3:20). The universal perspective of the book is further emphasized in that the book starts with a universal perspective of doom upon the whole of creation but ends with a universal perspective of restoration and salvation.

Zephaniah is a prophet of hope. Even in the midst of idolatry, foreign religious rituals, mistrust, violence, deceit and all kinds of injustices in society, there is the hope that YHWH will intervene on behalf of his people and restore them as a reconstituted people who will enjoy the presence and love of YHWH. It is a book that is worthy to be read and appreciated.

ANALYSIS

A. Superscription (1:1)
B. Universal judgment and (maybe) salvation (1:2 – 2:3)
  i. Universal judgment is announced (1:2–3)
  ii. Judgment upon Judah and Jerusalem (1:4–6)
  iii. Judgment because of the sins committed by the covenant people (1:7–13)
  iv. Judgment on the Day of YHWH and (perhaps) salvation (1:14 – 2:3)
C. Judgment upon the other nations as well (2:4–15)
D. Universal judgment and salvation (3:1–20)
  i. Judgment announced upon Jerusalem (3:1–8)
  ii. Salvation announced to the nations (3:9–13)
  iii. A call to joy because God is with his people (3:14–20)

COMMENTARY

A. Superscription (1:1)

Context

The context of the book is provided in its heading stating that the prophecies contained in it are to be related to the time of Josiah, king of Judah (*c.*640–609 BC).

Comment

1. The book of Zephaniah commences in a way familiar from other prophetic books (Jer. 1:2; Hos. 1:1; Joel 1:1; Jon. 1:1; Mic. 1:1; Hag. 1:1; Zech. 1:1; Mal. 1:1) by announcing the content of the book that follows as 'The word of YHWH'. It is at once clear that what one can expect are not the thoughts or ideas of just another human being; what follows has to be considered as the word of YHWH and thus as divine revelation.

The word of YHWH is revealed to people by human agents – in the case of the book of Zephaniah, by a person named *Zephaniah*. Nothing else is added so that we might know more about the person behind the book. We are not informed whether or not he was married (as was the case with Isaiah and Hosea), had children (as was the case with Isaiah, in Isa. 7:3; 8:3, and Hosea), where he came from (as for Amos, who came from Tekoa) or what age he was when he was called to be a prophet. His name means 'YHWH hides' or 'YHWH has hidden', or perhaps 'YHWH has preserved or protected', but that does not tell the reader anything significant about his background. There is also no obvious relationship between the meaning of the name of the prophet and the content of the book named after him. The proper noun *Zephaniah* occurs elsewhere in the Old Testament. In 1 Chronicles 6:36 a Zephaniah is mentioned as an ancestor of Heman, a Levitical musician (1 Chr. 6:33).

Jeremiah 21:1 identifies another Zephaniah as a priest. In Zechariah 6:10 a third Zephaniah is found, referred to as the father of Josiah, the high priest in Jerusalem after the exile. The name is thus not that uncommon in Israel/Judah and the links with the priesthood and Levitical circles are noteworthy. None of these other persons named Zephaniah can be identified with or related to Zephaniah the prophet introduced here in verse 1.

Unique to the book is the way in which he is introduced. In no other prophetic book is a prophet introduced by way of a genealogy going back no fewer than four generations (*Cushi, Gedaliah, Amariah, Hezekiah*). Zephaniah's father is given as *Cushi*. Cush in the Old Testament refers to the southern part of Egypt, the area known today as Ethiopia. It is a matter of dispute whether this is simply the name of his father or indicates his nationality as somebody coming from Cush. The name of Cushi's father, however, is *Gedaliah*, clearly a Judean name, making it unlikely that Zephaniah's father was a Cushite. In later times a man bearing the name of Gedaliah was appointed governor in Judah during the Babylonian rule (Jer. 40 – 41). Next in Zephaniah's ancestral lineage was *Amariah*, of whom nothing is known. The last name is *Hezekiah*, the great-great-grandfather of Zephaniah. On hearing the name of Hezekiah, one immediately thinks of Hezekiah the king of Judah (725–696 BC). Was the purpose of the extended genealogy of Zephaniah to prove that this prophet was of royal descent? Hezekiah is known as a good king, and King Josiah is known for his reforms, so the mention of Hezekiah creates a nice link between two good, God-fearing kings in the troubled history of God's people. However, if Hezekiah the king is intended, then the question arises as to why he is not specified as the king. Furthermore, according to 2 Kings 21 – 22, only two generations separated Hezekiah from Josiah (Manasseh and Amon), not three as is indicated here. Also, Amariah is not known to have been one of Hezekiah's sons. Finally, Hezekiah does occur elsewhere in the Old Testament as a proper noun (1 Chr. 3:23; Ezra 2:16; Neh. 7:21). The real reasons for the extended genealogy still elude us, as Hezekiah here does not appear to refer to the king.

The last part of the verse informs the reader that Zephaniah prophesied *during the reign of Josiah, king of Judah*. King Josiah is known as the king who introduced far-reaching reforms after the disastrous reigns of his predecessors (cf. the Introduction).

Meaning

As in the other prophetic books, what we have in this book is God's speech in human language. How exactly God revealed his message to human beings remains a mystery. The text informs us that the word (literally) 'happened to Zephaniah'. YHWH is the God who speaks to his people in difficult times, and he does so through prophets called to proclaim the word they have received from YHWH.

The historical framework of this first verse is important for the message in the book. YHWH's message brought by his prophet was meant for a specific time in the history of God's people. Precisely because this word of YHWH was addressed to a specific period in history, it can also speak to his people in other periods of time.

B. Universal judgment and (maybe) salvation (1:2 – 2:3)

i. Universal judgment is announced (1:2–3)

Context

Verses 2–3 form an *inclusio*. This section starts with a pronouncement that YHWH will sweep away everything *from the face of the earth*, and it ends with a similar pronouncement that humans will be cut off *from the face of the earth*.

Comment

2–3. The actual prophecy starts with a universal message. A literal rendering of the verb in Hebrew (*'sp*) used here has the meaning 'to gather'. Everything will be gathered by YHWH. Just as the harvest on farmland is harvested or gathered in so that nothing is left behind, so YHWH will gather in everything on earth with nothing left behind. The entire earth will experience total destruction. This proclamation of universal judgment echoes what once happened in Genesis 6 when God also said that everything (humans, animals, creatures that move along the ground, birds) would be wiped from the face of the earth (Gen. 6:7). This is affirmed by the solemn 'oracle of YHWH' (NIV *declares the LORD*). Divine authority is at work. Creation will be undone.

Verse 3 continues the message of total and utter destruction by making use of the same verb. YHWH will *sweep away* humans, animals, birds and fish, adding detail to the initial threat of sweeping away *everything.*

Meaning

The book starts off with a majestic picture of YHWH as the universal judge of the whole of creation. YHWH is indeed the almighty Creator God who has the power also to undo his creation. Although it is not said, it is clear that the animals, birds and fish are not the reason for this terrible announcement of total destruction; it can only be human beings who are the guilty ones. They are the reason for this proclamation of doom upon the whole of creation. More specifically, it is the wicked who are to blame for this coming judgment. We as the inhabitants of the creation are in a similar way the reason why creation has to suffer, because of our sinful behaviour.

ii. Judgment upon Judah and Jerusalem (1:4–6)
Context

After the announcement of universal judgment, attention shifts to Judah. Judah is accused of worshipping Baal and astral deities while still worshipping YHWH. Verse 5 is structured as an antithetic parallelism: (A) *those who bow down . . . to worship the starry host,* (A) *those who bow down and* (B) *swear by* YHWH, *and who . . . swear by Molech* (B). Over against those who bow down to worship the host of heaven and swear by the foreign god Molech stand those who worship YHWH and swear by his name.

Comment

4. The announcement of the coming judgment is now narrowed down to Judah and the capital, Jerusalem. Impending judgment is made clear by the opening phrase of this unit: YHWH will *stretch out* his *hand against* his people. In the past YHWH had led them from Egypt with an outstretched hand (Exod. 7:5, 19; 9:22; 14:16, 26). This figure of salvation may also indicate YHWH's judgment (Isa. 14:26–27; Ezek. 14:13; 16:27; 35:3). Just as humankind in general will

be cut off from the face of the earth, so Judah and the inhabitants
of Jerusalem will be cut off from *this place* (presumably the capital),
as will all that remains of Baal worship. The *priests* who serve the
idols will also be destroyed, even to the extent that they will have
no descendants. Baal was the god of fertility and therefore deemed
to be responsible for a good harvest from the land. The people will
once again have to acknowledge the one and only God. It is YHWH,
the covenant God, who meets the needs of his people, not Baal, the
supposed fertility god.

5–6. Verse 5 addresses syncretistic practices among the people.
While they keep worshipping YHWH, they also worship heavenly
bodies like the sun, moon and stars (*the starry host*). Evidence of
worshipping astral deities is found in the book of Kings (2 Kgs
21:3, 5, 21; 23:5, 12) during the reigns of Manasseh and Amon and
part of the time of Josiah. This was a direct violation of the first
and second commandments (Exod. 20:2–5). In fact, the same verb
(*bow down*) used in verse 5 is used in Exodus 20:5. In Deuteronomy
4:19 the people of God are admonished not to bow down to the
sun, moon and stars. The syncretistic practices are illustrated in a
particularly sharp way by using the same verb 'to bow down' for
both the worship of the astral bodies and the worship of YHWH. It
is interesting to note that it is explicitly said that the astral deities are
worshipped *on the roofs*. Presumably the worship of these deities
took place at night when especially the moon and stars would have
been more visible. It is also possible that worshipping them on the
roofs would bring the people closer to these gods. Molech was
known as an Ammonite god (1 Kgs 11:5, 33; 2 Kgs 23:13). Just as
God's people *swear by* YHWH, they also *swear by* Molech. The sin the
people have committed is not that they have forsaken YHWH as
their God but rather that they worship other, foreign gods as well.
Because God demands exclusive worship, their worship of other
gods means that they have *turn[ed] back from following* YHWH. They
will not trust YHWH alone. The people of God have lost faith in
God. To *seek* God means to worship him, and to *enquire of him* has
the meaning of seeking guidance from him. It speaks of a true relationship with God, of committing oneself to him and to him alone,
of devoting oneself to him in prayer and awaiting guidance for
the decisions to be made in life. To seek God and to enquire of him

are testimonies of devotion to God, but the people are no longer
doing so.

Meaning

God demands exclusive worship from his people. This was revealed
to them back at Mount Sinai in the Decalogue, it was reiterated
countless times in the rest of the Torah, and prophet after prophet
spoke about it in the course of their history. Yet Judah still gave in
to the temptation to worship other gods, especially the fertility god
of Canaan, Baal. Little wonder, then, that this prophet is also called
to speak out and reprimand the people once again to repent of their
sinful practices.

iii. Judgment because of the sins committed by the covenant people (1:7–13)

Context

Demarcating this unit is problematic. It seems as if verse 7 does not
fit in well between verses 4–6 and 8–9 and should therefore be
shifted to the beginning of verse 14 where the theme of the Day
of YHWH is introduced. Another view is that verse 7 should be
seen as an independent unit, standing on its own (Elliger 1975: 62;
Seybold 1985: 23–24; House 1988: 58). There is, however, good
reason to see verses 7–13 as a separate unit. In verses 4–6 first-
person singular forms dominate, whereas in verses 7–13 there is a
shift to third-person singular forms. Verse 7 introduces the theme
of the Day of YHWH in the book – an important indication that
verse 7 functions as the beginning of a new unit. The imperative
Be silent before the Sovereign YHWH is another indication of a new unit.
Terms connected with time are prominent (vv. 8, 10, 12) and serve
as another argument for taking verses 7–13 as a unit. No fewer than
three times the verb 'to visit' (though translated as *punish*) is found
(vv. 8, 9 and 12). In verse 14 the phrase 'Day of YHWH is near' is
repeated, thereby introducing another aspect of the expected day
of YHWH's decisive intervention. Verses 8–9, 10–11 and 12–13 are
marked by temporal clauses (*on that day*), grouping the unit into
three different parts, while verse 7 serves as an introduction to the
unit as a whole. The verb 'to visit' (*punish*) occurring in verses 8, 9
and 12 then binds the different parts together into a single unit.

The unit culminates in verse 13 with an announcement of judgment upon those whose sins have been described in the previous
verses. Historically speaking, it is safe to date the text to the years
preceding the reforms initiated by Josiah in 622 BC.

Comment

7. *Be silent* is a call to be silent in the presence of YHWH as a sign
of awe and respect. The call to be silent has a cultic or liturgical
setting in this case (Amos 6:10; Hab. 2:20; Zech. 2:13) with the
expectation of a mighty theophany of YHWH. This theophany will
manifest itself on the 'Day of YHWH' which is at hand. The idea of
a theophany also brings the Sinai tradition to mind as the coming
of YHWH in a theophany is closely associated with the events at
Mount Sinai (Snyman 2000b: 94). The earliest reference to the Day
of YHWH is in Amos 5:18 and it is a term found only in the prophetic literature of the Old Testament. The term was known in
Israel/Judah and the positive expectation was that it would be a
time of decisive intervention by YHWH when the enemies of the
people of God would be punished and effectively destroyed, while
it would be a day of salvation for the people of God. In the prophetic literature this popular view is turned around: the Day of
YHWH will also be a day of judgment for the people of God. The
theme of the Day of YHWH introduced here is an important theme
in the rest of the book.

Closely connected to the announcement of the coming Day
of YHWH is the announcement of a *sacrifice* prepared by YHWH to
be shared with those he has called to attend this sacrificial meal.
The surprising aspect in this announcement is that it will not
be Judah participating in the sacrificial feast but other nations,
with Judah as the sacrifice. There is also a nice ambiguity contained
in the text. The Hebrew word used for *sacrifice* has the meaning
of a sacrificial meal eaten in communion with YHWH. The same
verb also has the meaning of 'slaughter'. The text thus reveals a
kind of double meaning: while a sacrificial meal is prepared it will
at the same also be a slaughtering. To the utter shock and amazement of the people, YHWH will call others as guests and *consecrate*
them to take part in the sacrificial meal, while they will be
slaughtered.

8–9. Verse 8 follows logically from verse 7 as both the themes of the coming Day of YHWH and the sacrifice are taken up. The use of the first-person singular form indicates that YHWH is now speaking. He will punish the leading figures or the royal advisers, the royal household as well as others wearing *foreign clothes*. Exactly why foreign garments are the reason for punishment is not at once clear. It may be that *foreign clothes* refers to following the latest fashion trends from other cultures. The question arises whether that would be a sin worthy of the harsh punishment hinted at in the previous verse. To dress in foreign clothing may have a religious connotation. In 2 Kings 10:22 Jehu ordered the keeper of the wardrobe to bring robes for all the ministers of Baal, after which Jehu, together with Jehonadab, went into the temple of Baal and made sacrifices and burnt offerings with the ministers of Baal (2 Kgs 10:24). Special clothing was, then, associated with the worship of Baal. Since syncretistic religious practices were addressed in 1:4–6 and are again referred to in verse 9, it seems that that is the case here as well.

Verse 9 refers to an odd custom of leaping over the *threshold* of a temple. Popular belief held that divine figures had been buried under the thresholds and that those who wished to worship had to jump over the threshold to avoid the influence of these figures. Information on this custom is provided in 1 Samuel 5:4–5. The ark of God had been taken to Ashdod and set beside an image of Dagon, the Philistine god, in Dagon's temple. The second morning after the ark was placed there, Dagon was found fallen down before the ark, with his head and hands 'broken off and . . . lying on the threshold'. Then it is added, 'That is why . . . neither the priests of Dagon nor any others who enter Dagon's temple at Ashdod step on the threshold' (1 Sam. 5:5). This strange custom thus has its origin in foreign religious superstitious practices that apparently have now been adopted by the priests. Once again it is syncretistic religious practices that are criticized by the prophet.

The second part of the verse refers to an issue concerning social justice. The phrase 'house/temple of their lords/gods' is a *crux interpretum*. Does the phrase refer to the temple? That is unlikely because it is difficult to see how 'their masters/lords' can refer to

God. It seems improbable that the prophet would speak of *their* God instead of *our* God. Once again, one has to allow for ambiguity in the text. In Jerusalem, the temple complex and the palace of the king were attached and therefore seen as one complex. The accusation brought against the people is that the house of the rulers is filled with goods obtained by means of *violence and deceit*.

10–11. The sacrifice and slaughtering (v. 7) of Jerusalem are described from a geographical point of view in verses 10–11. There is also a shift from the religious matters addressed in verses 7–9 to commercial matters, and how the sacrifice will have an effect on the economic activity of the city. The text, taken literally, says that the 'sound of a cry' will be heard. A particularly strong word is used for *cry*, one that denotes the idea of crying for help. *Wailing* also describes the sound of people in pain, while the sound of a *loud crash* probably refers to the sound of collapsing walls and buildings. It may also have the connotation of screaming in intense distress. The *Fish Gate* was situated to the north of the city (Neh. 3:3), the most likely side from which an attack from an enemy could be expected. The *New Quarter* (2 Kgs 22:14), as the name suggests, indicates a more recent part of the city, and it is the next section of the city to fall after the Fish Gate is taken. The *hills* probably refers to an area within the city and not the surrounding hills outside the city. The 'Mortar' (NIV margin; or *market district*) is associated with that part of the city known for its economic activity, hence the mention of *merchants* and those who *trade with silver*. Utter destruction, total devastation, awaits the city.

12–13. Verse 12 makes the coming judgment even clearer: when YHWH comes at the time of judgment he will *search Jerusalem with lamps*. Searching the city with lamps indicates the thoroughness of YHWH's investigation. Nothing will be hidden and nobody will be able to hide in dark corners from YHWH's search. Those who are *complacent* are compared to impure *wine*. In the process of winemaking the impurities (called *dregs* or lees) that have sunk to the bottom must be removed. If this is not done, these impurities will have a devastating effect on the quality of the wine, making it an undrinkable, sour and jelly-like concoction.

The attitude exposed by the prophet is a frightening one. According to the people's thinking, God simply does not matter any more. The figure of merism is used to indicate totality: *do nothing, either good or bad* means he does nothing at all. Although YHWH is present, he is inactive. It is not the question of God's existence that is at stake; it is God's active involvement in history that is being questioned. Verse 13 serves as a summary of the preceding verses. *Wealth* acquired will be looted and *plundered*. All their hard work of building *houses* and planting *vineyards* will not succeed. Wealth, houses and vineyards are blessings the people of God may enjoy because they are taken up in a covenant relationship with God. When the people turn away from God, it follows that they will also forfeit the blessings associated with the covenant. Those who have declared themselves independent of God will find that their new-found 'security' does not provide the security and well-being they thought it would. The God who according to their thinking is inactive is very much at work after all: the total devastation that awaits them will be an experience for them of YHWH's active involvement in their lives.

Meaning

In the Old Testament in general and in this unit in particular, it is important to keep in mind that the announcement of judgment is also a call to repentance. The doom of judgment announced is not YHWH's final word. Should the people pay attention to the announcement of judgment and repent, there will be no judgment.

YHWH demands exclusive worship. He is the one and only God and he cannot tolerate syncretistic practices – the incorporation of the worship of other gods. At the same time, social injustices are addressed as well. When rulers enrich themselves by means of violence and deceit it is ethically wrong, and the prophet unmasks this type of human conduct in vivid language.

Religious indifference is also unmasked by the prophet in this unit. While people insist that they still worship YHWH, they practise all kinds of superstitious religious customs foreign to, and in fact in contradiction of, the worship of YHWH.

This kind of religious indifference is summarized by the prophet in verse 12 when he describes people as not caring about God because they perceive him to be inactive, doing neither good nor bad. One should be careful not to impose modern Western

concepts of atheism or agnosticism onto the text. Neither the existence of God nor the fact that he may be known is questioned; what
is questioned is his active involvement in the lives and history of
his people.

iv. Judgment on the Day of YHWH and (perhaps) salvation (1:14 – 2:3)

Context

Verses 14–18 are considered one of the masterpieces of poetry in
the Old Testament. Reading this unit in Hebrew reveals a number
of alliterations and end rhymes. The term 'day' occurs no less than
ten times in these verses. Verse 7 began with an announcement that
the Day of YHWH is near, and verse 14 begins with the same
announcement. This unit is also marked by wordplay in the Hebrew
language, where words that sound similar are used; however, this
is almost impossible to reproduce in a translation.

Chapter 2:1–3 concludes the unit by offering a glimmer of
hope in the midst of the announcement of judgment upon the
people. Motyer (1998: 926) detected a chiastic structure in this last
part of the unit: (A) verse 1 is a summons to assemble; (B) verse 2
consists of a threefold ground for urgency; (B') verse 3a–c consists of a threefold command to seek; followed by verse 3d (A')
as a motivation where a possible shelter from YHWH's anger is
foreseen.

There is no evidence from the unit to determine a historical date
for the prophecy.

Comment

14. Verse 14 repeats verse 7, with the exception that *great* is
added, to read: *The great day of* [YHWH] *is near*. Also added is that the
day is *near and coming quickly*. This addition suggests a sense of
urgency with no time to waste. The second half of the verse
consists of only seven words in the Hebrew language, yet it is
difficult to translate these words in an adequate way. The NIV
translates:

> *The cry on the day of the* LORD *is bitter;*
>   *the Mighty Warrior shouts his battle cry.*

The NRSV translates it as:

> the sound of the day of the LORD is bitter,
>   the warrior cries aloud there.

It is also possible to translate these words as interjections and exclamations, as follows:

> Listen! The day of YHWH! How bitter!
>   A warrior shouts out there!

The GNT translates: 'That day will be bitter, for even the bravest soldiers will cry out in despair!' Whatever the case may be, the message the text wants to communicate is that the coming Day of YHWH will be a bitter event, so much so that even a warrior or soldier will cry out. The word used for *warrior* describes a particularly brave and strong man. Even the bravest of men will cry out when the Day of YHWH arrives. In line with other prophets Zephaniah makes it clear that the coming Day of YHWH is not a day of deliverance for Judah and doom for the other nations; in fact, the day is described as *bitter* for Judah.

15–16. Verses 15–16 describe the Day of YHWH in no less than six brief and vivid phrases without making use of a main verb. This staccato-like structure adds to the sense of urgency already stated in verse 14. The rapid way in which the coming of the day is described makes it clear that no-one will escape from the terror of that day. The coming is described as a day of YHWH's *wrath*, *distress* or destruction, and *anguish*, *trouble* or destruction and *ruin* or devastation, *darkness and gloom, clouds and blackness* or deep darkness, *trumpet* and a *battle cry against the fortified cities*. It is especially the day being described as *darkness* that recalls the wonder of the deliverance from Egypt, when the ninth wonder was three days of darkness. What happened once to Egypt will now happen to the people who experienced redemption from the bondage of Egypt. The history of God's deliverance of his people is now turned against them as they will experience what Egypt once experienced. Every attempt at defending themselves will be to no avail.

17–18. The reason for this terrible event is made clear in verse 17: the people have *sinned against* YHWH. No further explanation is given as to what sins the prophet has in mind. In the previous unit (1:7–9) the sins named were their syncretistic religious practices and the way in which they acquired material wealth by means of violence and deceit. In the announcement of the coming judgment YHWH speaks in first-person singular forms and the message of doom is now also brought to the individual 'man' (*'ādām*). Is the designation of the people of God as 'man' (*'ādām*) a subtle indication that the covenantal relationship between God and his people has been broken with the result that they will now be considered as all other people? The distress that they are about to endure will leave them disoriented, like *blind* people trying to find their way in complete darkness.

The end result of the judgment will be utter humiliation. Their *blood* will be *like dust, poured out,* and – even worse – *their entrails* will be *like dung. Dust* and *dung* are both worthless and that is exactly what the people of God will be on the day of judgment – as worthless as dust and dung. What a terrible humiliation awaits the people of God!

Their wealth acquired in dubious ways (vv. 9, 11) will be to no avail when the day of YHWH's judgment arrives. In the previous unit (v. 13) it was said that the wealth the merchants acquired would be plundered. It was possible for a city or country to pay tribute to an invading army to save them from total annihilation. On the Day of YHWH, however, there will be no room for bargaining to make a deal like this with YHWH.

Chapter 1 (vv. 2–3) started with a universal perspective when it was announced that the whole of creation will suffer the judgment of YHWH. The last verse of the chapter returns to this universal perspective: *all who live on the earth* will come to *a sudden end*.

What motivated this prophetic announcement of universal judgment? Behind the harsh language of terrible judgment is YHWH, the *jealous* God of the covenant. It is YHWH who entered into a covenant relationship with his people in which exclusive worship is a *sine qua non*. When his people acted treacherously YHWH was left with almost no other option than to announce judgment upon them. The people will experience that YHWH is not inactive, doing nothing, as they had thought (v. 12). On the contrary, YHWH is active in the events about to happen to them. In 3:8 the announcement of judgment because of his zeal (or jealousy) for his people is repeated.

2:1–3. These next few verses offer a slight possibility of salvation from the coming Day of YHWH. This sub-unit starts off with two verbs from the same root in Hebrew calling upon the people to *gather* themselves. What is unusual about this call is that the verbs used are normally used for straw being gathered. Robertson (1990: 289–290) noted how this verb is used for the gathering of straw by the Israelites in Egypt (Exod. 5:7), the gathering of straw on the sabbath (Num. 15:32–33; NIV 'wood') and the gathering of straw by the widow in the time of Elijah (1 Kgs 17:10; NIV 'sticks'). The subtle nuance of this verb signals that the people of God are considered as nothing more than straw. It is also interesting that the word used to indicate the people of God is the word used in many cases in the Old Testament to describe the other nations. Once again there is a subtle play in the text that the people of God are no longer considered as such. They are like any other nation.

The second verb used in verse 1 is problematic. The verb (*kāsap* in Hebrew) can be translated as 'to grow pale' but can also, as in Job 14:15, be rendered 'to long for' or 'to desire'. If this is the case the meaning of the phrase will be that the nation of Judah is no longer considered as the people of God and also no longer desired by God. It is also possible that the verb says something about the people: they do not desire God or anything else. Another possibility is to render the verb as 'shame' or *shameful*, because one can be made pale by shame. In this sense the phrase would mean that Judah does not know any shame for the sins it has committed. Whichever choice is made, it is clear that the term is used in a derogatory manner. Judah does not desire God and/or does not show any shame for the sins it has committed, and in this way it has severely disrupted its relationship with YHWH. Much is being said about Judah in few words: Judah as a nation is considered as worthless straw, no longer the people of God and with no shame for the sins it has committed.

Verse 2 also presents the interpreter with problems. Especially the first half of the Hebrew text is difficult to understand or make sense of. The different translations proposed in Bible versions and commentaries are ample proof of the difficulty in achieving a proper understanding of this text. The NIV translates this verse as

> *before the decree takes effect*
> *and that day passes like windblown chaff.*

The NRSV translates it as:

> before you are driven away
> like the drifting chaff.

The GNT has the following rendering: 'before you are driven away like chaff blown by the wind'; Robertson (1990: 289): 'Before the decree gives birth (like chaff the day passes over)'; and Motyer (1998: 925): 'Before the decree takes effect, like chaff clear gone all at once.'

The Day of YHWH has been announced and it will come. But the day has not come yet. There is thus time between the announcement of the coming judgment and the day of judgment. There is, however, very little time left – time that will elapse like chaff blown away by the wind. The sense of urgency in the call is emphasized by the threefold appearance of *before*.

The second part of the verse underlines the terrible and fearsome day of YHWH's anger and wrath. The Day of YHWH will be a time of judgment but it will come only if the people have not responded to the many calls from the prophet to repent and turn back to YHWH.

Verse 3 is a powerful statement in the book as a whole. Where verse 2 was characterized by the threefold *before* (*before the decree, before the LORD's fierce anger, before the day of the LORD's wrath*) warning the people of the coming judgment, verse 3 is characterized by a threefold *seek* (*Seek the LORD, Seek righteousness, seek humility*), opening up a slight possibility of salvation. Verse 3 addresses a different audience from that addressed in the previous verses. Verse 1 addressed the *shameful nation*, but in verse 3 the *humble of the land* are addressed. The *humble of the land* are those who have remained faithful to YHWH. The humble people stand in stark contrast to those who are complacent, thinking that YHWH is inactive and not involved in their situation any more (1:12).

Earlier in the book (1:6) one of the accusations was that the people did not seek YHWH; now they are summoned to indeed *seek* him. To *seek* YHWH means to turn to YHWH in sincere worship, praying to him and asking for his guidance, in deep dependence on him. In the light of the previous prophetic speeches denouncing syncretistic worship practices, this will mean worshipping YHWH exclusively, as stipulated in the Decalogue.

The humble of the land are encouraged not only to worship YHWH but also to practise *righteousness* in their conduct with other people. The terms 'justice' and 'righteousness' are often used together in the Old Testament. Both of these terms have general human conduct in mind. Justice is not a theoretical concept: it is something to be done, something practised in a believer's day-to-day contact with others. In contrast to those who engage in foreign religious practices and increase their material possessions through violence and deceit (1:9) are the humble of the land who do justice. There is no tension between seeking YHWH and doing justice; in fact, to serve YHWH in worship and prayer and to do justice are two sides of the same coin. All of this is accomplished in true *humility* in relation both to God and to other human beings.

What does 'justice' (*mišpāṭ*) actually mean? According to Koehler and Baumgartner (1958: 579–580) this term denotes a decision or judgment, especially within the legal sphere, and therefore it pertains to a decision taken in terms of judgment. Justice may then also mean 'a case presented for judgment' (*THAT* 2: 1002), denoting a legal and just decision. Justice happens when the disrupted social order in society has been restored. 'Justice' is therefore a term not to be restricted to the legal sphere; it may also have the meaning of 'that which is one's due, which is one's right, what one is entitled to' (*THAT* 2: 1005). Wright (2004: 257) comes to a similar conclusion when he describes justice as 'what needs to be done in a given situation if people and circumstances are to be restored to conformity with righteousness'. Throughout the Old Testament/ Hebrew Bible there is an almost unquestioned conviction that YHWH is the God of justice (Deut. 4:5–8; Ps. 89:14; Isa. 30:18).

Righteousness is a well-known concept in the Old Testament/ Hebrew Bible, and von Rad's view on this term, quoted above in the commentary on Habakkuk 2:4, is worth noting again: 'There is absolutely no concept in the Old Testament with so central a significance for all the relationships of human life as that of right- eousness' (von Rad 1975: 370). The term indicates a relationship between two parties that is in order, meaning that a particular rela- tionship conforms to the expectations one may have of it (Wright 2004: 256). Righteousness is disrupted by war or quarrels, and when such disruption happens, the relationship must be restored. Right- eousness is also something to be done in practical terms, displaying the appropriate behaviour in a relationship by meeting the accepted standards. Von Rad (1975: 374) reminds us that it would 'be an utterly false description of the facts' to think of righteousness as either a secular (human relationships) or religious (human beings with God) concept; rather they 'were bound together'. Righteous- ness is a term closely connected to justice.

Do coming before God in an attitude of sincere worship, practising justice and having restored human relationships guar- antee one against the anger of YHWH on the day of judgment? The answer to this question is clear from the text: by no means can one rely on one's own religious customs and practices, however sincere they may be. God's salvation of his people cannot be forced from him. He is and remains the sovereign God. The only way even the humble of the land may be rescued from the disaster awaiting the people is by the grace of God. *Perhaps* a remnant will escape the terrible judgment of YHWH.

The command to seek YHWH is reminiscent of Amos 5:6, 14–15, where the people are also summoned to seek YHWH. Although different verbs are used, the humble of the land needing to seek justice and humility is also reminiscent of Micah 6:8, where it is required of believers to do justice, to love mercy and to walk humbly with God.

Meaning
God will come to judge his people on the Day of YHWH – that is made abundantly clear in vivid poetic language. The reason for the imminent judgment is also stated in clear terms: the people are

guilty of religious syncretistic practices and of acquiring wealth by means of violence and deceit. YHWH has entered into a covenant relationship with his people and therefore he is zealous to keep the relationship intact. YHWH is not the inactive God they think he is (1:12); he is very much active, as will become apparent when the time for judgment arrives. Yet God's wrath is not the final word. Even though his covenant people are now regarded as just another nation and as worthless as straw, there is still the slight possibility that the judgment may be averted. There is still a little time that is not to be wasted between the announcement of judgment and the judgment itself in the awesome Day of YHWH. True religion means to worship YHWH alone and to do justice according to the commandments of God. However, even sincere religion can offer no guarantee of salvation. Salvation can come only from YHWH.

God is revealed in this passage as both the righteous God and the gracious God. His righteousness demands that because of their sins his people should suffer his wrath in punishment. Yet, at the same time, God's graciousness demands that it should still be possible for the people who humble themselves and repent not to experience judgment. The divine *perhaps* suggesting the possibility of salvation instead of judgment is found elsewhere in the Book of the Twelve as well (Joel 2:14; Amos 5:15; Jon. 3:9). In the New Testament Jesus is known for his humility (Matt. 11:29; 21:5).

C. Judgment upon the other nations as well (2:4–15)

Context
Zephaniah 2:4–15 consists of prophecies of judgment against well-known foreign peoples: Philistia (2:4–7), Moab and Ammon (2:8–11), Cush (2:12) and finally Assyria (2:13–15). Prophecies against foreign nations are not uncommon in the prophetic literature of the Old Testament. They are found in the major prophetic books of Isaiah, Jeremiah and Ezekiel (Isa. 13 – 23; Jer. 46 – 51; Ezek. 25 – 32) as well as in all the books of the Book of the Twelve except Hosea. With 3:1 the prophecy is once again directed towards Jerusalem.

It is significant that the unit commences with an emphatic 'For' (NRSV) or 'Indeed' (*kî*) in the Hebrew text. On the one hand, it is clear that verses 4–15 can be separated from verses 1–3, but on the other hand, the emphatic 'for' in verse 4 does connect the prophecies of doom on foreign nations with the prophecy against Judah. Judah is called a nation in 2:1 on the same level, so to speak, as the foreign nations, and in verse 4 prophecies against foreign nations follow the prophecy against Judah. The Day of YHWH will be an event that affects not only the people of God but indeed all nations worldwide. The far-reaching extent of the judgment of God can be seen from a geographical point as well. Philistia, Moab and Ammon are nations near to Judah, while Cush and Assyria are far away.

The first sub-unit also concludes with 'For' in verse 7 (NRSV), creating an *inclusio* with verse 4 and thereby bracketing these verses as a separate unit within the larger context of 2:4–15. In verse 8 Moab and Ammon are addressed while in verse 12 Cush is addressed. Verses 8–11 are, then, to be considered as the next sub-unit. In verses 13–15 Assyria is addressed, bracketing this sub-unit within the broader unit of 2:4–15.

No indication is given as to why these prophecies of judgment are pronounced against Philistia (vv. 4–7) and Cush (v. 12). In the case of Moab and Ammon they are accused of making insults and taunting the people of God, and in the case of Assyria their hubris (v. 15) is given as the reason for the verdict upon them.

Comment

4–7. Four of the five well-known cities of Philistia are mentioned (*Gaza, Ashkelon, Ashdod, Ekron*; Gath is omitted). The sequence in which the cities are named is interesting: Gaza is the city farthest south from Judah, Ashkelon and Ashdod are located more to the north, while Ekron is the closest to Judah. The verbs used to describe the fate of these cities indicate complete and utter destruction. Why it is said that Ashdod will be *emptied* at *midday* is not clear. The most plausible explanation is that an attack at midday will hold an element of surprise as midday is usually the time of siesta and relaxation. Another possibility is that the city will already have been taken by midday and its citizens removed. The main emphasis, however, remains on the total devastation that awaits the cities of Philistia. Gaza will have no inhabitants, Ashkelon will be desolated,

Ashdod will also be left with no inhabitants, and Ekron will be *uprooted* and consequently its people will be driven out of the city. Cities were considered to be safe places because of their fortifications and watchtowers, but on the Day of YHWH they will all be devastated.

Verse 5 continues the pronouncement of judgment on Philistia introduced by a term used at funerals to call people to lament. The verse is structured as a nice *inclusio*: it starts by calling upon those who inhabit the territory by the sea and it concludes by stating that there will be no inhabitants left in that part of the land. Here the term *Woe* is used to announce doom upon the Kerethites, a clan among the Philistines but in this case better understood to represent the whole of the nation of the Philistines. To call the Philistines 'Kerethites' refers to their geographical links with the island of Crete and this is also found elsewhere in the Old Testament (1 Sam. 30:14; 2 Sam. 15:18; Ezek. 25:16). The Philistines were known as the people living *by the sea* and are addressed as such. The threatening tone of the prophecy is clear: 'the word of YHWH' is *against* them, indicating a verdict, and that means that they will be destroyed, with no-one left. It is also interesting to note that the Philistines are addressed as *Canaan* to indicate the land they occupied and to identify them with that land. Verse 6 makes it clear that the territory once occupied by the Philistines will be so completely devastated that it will now serve as a place for *shepherds* and sheep pens. Territory once used for commercial activities will now only be fit for *pastures* feeding sheep. While the prophecy will be bad news for the Philistines, it will be good news for the people of Judah: the land once occupied by the Philistines will now be used as pastures for sheep belonging to Judah. The last verse of this sub-unit brings an awkward twist to the prophecy. The punishment of the Philistines will result in the restoration of the *remnant* of Judah. In contrast to the devastation foreseen for the Philistines, a picture of peace is painted for the remnant. They will find pasture for their sheep and *In the evening* they will be able to *lie down* without any fear. This is all due to YHWH their God who will visit (1:8, 9, 12) them and *restore their fortunes*.

8–11. Moab and Ammon are next in the series of prophecies against foreign nations. Unlike verse 7, where YHWH was spoken of in the third-person singular form, now YHWH is speaking, in first-person singular form. As YHWH once heard the cry of distress of his people in Egypt (Exod. 2), so now he hears the *insults* and *taunts* from the Moabites and the Ammonites which are directed at his people. This insulting language was humiliating for the people. In particular, it is said that threats have been made *against their land*, meaning that the remnant probably lost some of the land once promised to them to these two foreign nations. It is difficult if not impossible to pinpoint these accusations to a specific time in history. Their eventual fate is compared to what happened to the cities of *Sodom* and *Gomorrah* (Gen. 18 – 19). Mention of these two cities is important and deliberate. It recalls the events told in Genesis 19. Lot and his family were living in Sodom and Gomorrah. Two angels visited Lot, warning him about the coming destruction of the two cities. Lot's family fled just before the cities were destroyed by burning sulphur raining down from heaven. Lot and his daughters settled on the outskirts of the small town of Zoar, living in a cave in the mountains. As both daughters were unmarried, they devised a plan to get pregnant by their father. Thus the elder daughter had a son by the name of Moab and the younger daughter had a son by the name of Ammon. These two sons became the ancestors of the Moabites and the Ammonites. On the one hand, then, the Moabites and Ammonites were related to the people of God, as Lot was a relative of Abraham. On the other hand, they were descendants of the incest between Lot and his daughters. There was also a long history of enmity and strife between Israel/Judah and these two nations (Num. 22:3; 1 Sam. 11:1–2; 2 Sam. 10:1–4; Neh. 4:3; Jer. 40:14). By recalling this event Zephaniah is saying that history is going to repeat itself. Just as Sodom and Gomorrah were destroyed, the descendants of the people who once lived there will also be destroyed.

While Moab and Ammon will suffer the judgment of YHWH, the *remnant* will be restored. Just as the people once took possession of the land, so they *will inherit* the land once more. Land that was lost will be returned to them. There will be a dramatic reversal of fortunes: Moab and Ammon, who once insulted the people of God, will be humiliated, while the people who once had to suffer their insults and mockery will be restored.

Verse 11 opens up an unexpected and completely fresh perspective. The focus is broadened from Moab and Ammon to a universal one in which it is envisaged that nations on every shore will worship YHWH. The focus also shifts from Moab and Ammon insulting the people of God to God acting against foreign gods. While God is to be feared, the gods are weak. The fear of God means that he is an *awesome* God, superior to any other god, mighty in power and respected by all. When the other gods are diminished into nothingness, nations will turn to God. The Hebrew word used to describe the eventual fate of the gods means 'to make thin'. The gods will wither away and become nothing. When the nations realize that worshipping their gods is an exercise in futility, they will turn to YHWH and start worshipping him. Since this prophecy was directed at the people of God, this message would have reminded them that they did the same as the foreign nations. The futility of worshipping other gods also applies to them as the people of God.

12. In a brief prophecy consisting of only six words in the Hebrew, the *Cushites* are addressed. Why Cush is named in this series of prophecies against foreign nations is not clear. Cush can be located south of Judah and was a far-off country in Africa that did not really present a threat to Judah. No sin is mentioned either. As Roberts (1991: 202) stated: 'We simply do not know what provoked this oracle.' In the other prophecies of doom upon foreign nations it is said that their land will be lost to them. Here it is simply stated that the Cushites will be pierced by *my sword* – an indication that YHWH will be the one who carries the sword and that they will be slain in a military confrontation. The prophecy is in line with the universal perspective of the previous oracle, again making it clear that the coming judgment will cover the whole world, as was already indicated right at the beginning of the book.

13–15. Assyria is the last in the series of foreign nations addressed by the prophet. In the second part of verse 13 *Nineveh*, the capital of Assyria, is mentioned as well. Nineveh will be made a desolation. A stark contrast is painted: Nineveh, a city located on the Tigris River and known for its canals, will become like a *desert*. The coming destruction will be so complete that nobody will survive. The country and its capital will be devoid of people and will be inhabited by domestic and wild animals. At night the eerie *hooting* of owls that nest on the *columns* will be heard. In stark contrast to the inhabitants' former claims that *there is none besides me*, the city will become a *ruin*. Indeed, in 612 BC the city was captured by the Medes and Babylonians and demolished. However, the downfall of Assyria cannot only be ascribed to a foreign military power. YHWH was at work, since it is he who

> *will stretch out his hand against the north*
>   *and destroy Assyria.*

The destruction was so complete that 'when the Greek traveller Xenophon visited the site in 401 BC, he could find no trace of it' (Clark and Hatton 1989: 177; see also Robertson 1990: 312). The unit forms an *inclusio* as it commences by mentioning the outstretched *hand* of YHWH and comes to a close by mentioning people passing by shaking their *fists* or waving their hands in disbelief.

Meaning

YHWH is not a local god restricted to one nation and territory; he is portrayed as the universal God with the authority and power to judge every nation on earth. Even more than that, God not only judges the nations of the world, but he also directs world history. The tyranny of a seemingly invincible world power would, and eventually did, come to an end.

YHWH will keep the covenant with his people, even though it may only be a remnant that will survive the judgment. This becomes clear when the previous prophecies against Judah are compared with these prophecies against the other nations in 2:4–15. Where total destruction was announced except for (perhaps!) a remnant, now the remnant will be in a position to occupy land. The Philistines as well as the Moabites and Ammonites will lose the land they occupied, while the remnant will occupy that very land. God acts on behalf of his people in spite of the threat other nations might be to them.

Yet, at the same time, this unit proclaims a remarkable universal perspective. Although YHWH is the *God of Israel* (v. 9) and they are *my people* (vv. 8, 9), a time is foreseen when *all the gods of the earth* will be destroyed and the nations will worship YHWH, *all of them in their own lands*. Elsewhere in the Old Testament (Isa. 2:2–4; Mic. 4:1–5; Zech. 14:16–19) it is envisaged that the nations will come to Jerusalem to worship. Here the remarkable perspective is that even people outside the land will worship YHWH.

D. Universal judgment and salvation (3:1–20)

i. Judgment announced upon Jerusalem (3:1–8)
Context

Chapter 3 introduces a new unit and a fresh emphasis. The very first word (*Woe* or 'alas') is indicative of the new emphasis. The woe oracle recalls a funeral lament and is intended to draw the attention of the audience. No indication is given as to who or what is addressed, but the mention of prophets and priests in verse 4, together with the accusation that violence is done to the law or Torah, makes it clear that Jerusalem is meant as *the city of oppressors* (v. 1). There are unfortunately no historical pointers to locate this oracle in history.

Demarcating the different sub-units in the chapter is problematic. In verse 8 a conclusion is drawn (*Therefore*) based upon the preceding prophecy, and 3:1–8 can be divided into two parts: verses 1–5 and 6–8. Verse 9 is then the introduction to the next sub-unit comprising promises of redemption and restoration. Verses 1–8 and 9–13 form a chiastic structure: (A) judgment upon Jerusalem (vv. 1–7); (B) judgment upon the nations (v. 8); (B′) salvation for the nations (v. 9); (A′) salvation for the people of God (vv. 11–13). The initial judgment upon Jerusalem (vv. 1–5) is contrasted with the announcement of salvation for the people of God (vv. 11–13). Likewise, after the initial announcement of judgment upon the nations (vv. 6–8), salvation is foreseen for them (vv. 9–10). The last part of the book consists of verses 14–20.

Comment

1. In 2:5 a woe oracle was used to introduce judgment on foreign nations. This time the woe oracle addresses the city of Jerusalem, with Jerusalem and its people placed on the same level as the foreign nations. That the first few verses of chapter 3 appear to

continue the judgment on Assyria and Nineveh underlines how the
people of God are treated the same as foreign nations. The simi-
larity drawn between Nineveh and Jerusalem must have been
shocking to the prophet's audience!

The city of Jerusalem is characterized by three participles –
rebellious, defiled and oppressive. *Rebellious* is taken as rebellion against
God through the disobedient behaviour of the people. Such
rebellious behaviour had a long history, going back to their very
beginning as the people of God and recalling the rebellion of the
people during the wanderings in the wilderness on their way from
Egypt to the Promised Land. Being *defiled* has the connotation of
personal defilement and refers to the sinful nature of individuals,
especially with regard to committing acts of violence. The reference
to oppression indicates that some people in powerful positions
have the power to oppress other people. Thus in only three words
the city's attitude towards God, self and other people is described
(Motyer 1998: 941).

2. Verse 2 piles up four accusations regarding things that the
city, and by implication the people, do not do. It is interesting to
note that second-person singular feminine verb forms are used:
She does not listen to the 'voice' (of God; NRSV), *she* does not accept
instruction or discipline, *she* does not put her *trust* in YHWH and *she*
does not *draw near* to God. The voice (presumably God's voice)
that the city does not listen to may refer to the voice of the
prophets proclaiming God's will for his people, or it may refer
to the Torah. In the well-known verse Deuteronomy 6:4, where
the same verb is used, the people are admonished to listen to the
requirements of the Torah. Earlier in the book of Deuteronomy
(4:33) the question is asked: 'Has any other people heard the voice
of God speaking out of fire, as you have, and lived?' The accusation that the people did not listen to the 'voice' means that they
did not obey the word of God that came to them via the prophetic
voices and/or the Torah of Moses. The term translated as 'discipline', *correction* or 'instruction' is predominantly found in the
wisdom literature of the Old Testament. As a term at home in
wisdom contexts, it denotes adhering to a way of life that accords
with the wisdom principles ordained by God. In Proverbs 6:23 it
is said that 'correction and instruction are the way to life'. Not

accepting discipline or instruction means that the people refuse to adhere to the stipulations of appropriate conduct. Here, by literally 'not taking correction', the people are accused of not taking seriously God's actions in the past to discipline them. In the past God disciplined them with the aim of correcting their ways according to his will.

The people are now reminded of what God did in the past. They are accused of not trusting YHWH. Putting one's trust in YHWH is a hallmark of believers often found in the Psalms (13:5; 25:2; 26:1). It is noteworthy that the covenant name of God is used here. The people are in a covenant relationship with God where unconditional trust is a *sine qua non*. Yet, in spite of the close covenantal relationship between YHWH and his people, they do not trust him. To not trust YHWH also means that they put their trust in other gods instead. The last accusation refers to the inner attitude of the people when they worship God. To worship God requires approaching him with a sincere heart. The people are no longer interested in approaching God to ask for help or to hear his word.

3–4. After addressing the city together with its inhabitants in general, the next verses focus on specific people both secular and religious in leadership positions in society. The royal *officials* or princes are likened to *roaring lions*. Lions that roar scare people and that is perhaps what the simile wants to communicate in the first place. Lions are predators that hunt and devour prey as they like. So the civil authorities act like lions ready to devour what is available to them. In similar vein, the 'judges' (NRSV; NIV *rulers*) are compared to *evening wolves* hunting. The prey are particularly vulnerable to predators during the night. Predators have the advantage of the dark of night, and the prey cannot spot predators as well as in the daytime. As with the lions, it is frightening to encounter a predator at night. When predators prey on an animal, they are known to feast on the carcass until the whole animal is devoured, with nothing left for the following day – not even the skin or bones in the case of a smaller antelope. Thus, instead of protecting people, providing leadership and making people feel safe in society, the opposite was happening. The officials and judges preyed on people like predators, so that the people were scared of them. The ordinary people's fear of the royal administrators is in line with the description given in verse 1 of the *city of oppressors*.

The religious leaders are also targeted. *Prophets* are described as arrogant and *treacherous* while the priests *profane* what is holy and *do violence* to the Torah. Acting in an arrogant way means that they are reckless and undisciplined in exercising their responsibilities as prophets. Instead of proclaiming the will of God, they can no longer be trusted and are therefore unmasked as deceivers. The priests are accused of profaning what is holy. They have little or no regard for their calling to oversee the sacrifices the people bring (Lev. 1 – 7; 19:8; Deut. 17:8–13). By their neglect the *sanctuary* is profaned. In this way they, together with the people, were bringing unworthy sacrifices that were defiled (as was indicated in v. 1). Another duty the priests had was to teach the Torah to the people. In their failure to do so, they did *violence* to the Torah, thereby doing violence to society. The priests are not accused of going astray to worship or offer sacrifices to other gods; it is the service rendered in their capacity as priests of YHWH that is under scrutiny by the prophet. To add to this, it has to be kept in mind that when what is holy is profaned it also has an effect on how the holiness of God is perceived, because what is regarded as holy is inevitably linked to the holiness of God. In Micah 3:9–12 the prophet also rebuked the leaders within society.

When the leaders in society act in this way it is nothing other than a practical manifestation of a rebellious life, as was indicated in verse 1. What the leaders do, the ordinary people will imitate, and, conversely, the moral fibre of people in society will be reflected in the conduct of those in leadership positions.

5. In stark contrast to the injustices committed by the leaders in society, YHWH's righteousness is emphasized. While society is characterized by injustices of all kinds, YHWH is in the midst of his sinful people as the *righteous* One who is incapable of doing anything wrong. In spite of all the wrongdoings of his people, YHWH stays committed to them as the righteous God. Where officials and rulers are compared to predators that devour their prey with nothing left in the morning (v. 3), YHWH's righteousness is dispensed *morning by morning*, day by day, indicating his continuous exercise of justice. Consequently, YHWH is one who can be trusted as the reliable God, and it is therefore better to draw near to him (v. 2). Again, where the corrupt leaders operate in the dark, like predators who devour their prey at night, YHWH's justice and righteousness will be experienced in the light of day (*Morning by morning . . . every new day*). YHWH can in no way be connected to the corrupt ways of the leaders and therefore it is said that *he does no wrong*. In contrast to YHWH's righteousness are the *unrighteous* who do not even feel *shame* for their misconduct. It is unthinkable that the leaders should simply continue with their unrighteous actions in the light of YHWH's righteousness; therefore the only conclusion is that they know no shame for their wrongdoing. In the Hebrew there is a nice play on words between YHWH who *does no wrong* and the 'wrongdoer' who has no shame. The contrast between the righteous YHWH and the unrighteous leaders couldn't be greater.

6–7. Strong language is used in verse 6 to describe YHWH's actions in the past against the nations. They have been cut off, their strongholds have been *demolished* and their *streets* have been left *deserted*. All of a sudden YHWH himself speaks in the first-person singular form. YHWH's deeds in history are recalled to remind the people what happened in the past. What happened in the past to other nations will happen to God's own people. What a terrible irony that the people of God are now compared to the other nations because there is so little difference in their behaviour. Nations have been cut off, strongholds in the form of towers at the corners of walls have been demolished and no people have been found on the cities' streets. Will history be a warning to the people to repent in order to avoid the same fate the nations suffered? This certainly was the expectation YHWH had of his people, according to verse 7. Once the people learn the lessons of history they will again turn to YHWH, *fear* him and *accept* the *correction* he wants them to take to heart. To *fear* YHWH means being in awe of his presence and respecting him as God of their lives. YHWH's correction is to the benefit of his people. Yet, contrary to the expectation that they would accept YHWH's correction, they have not done so, as verse 2 has already stated. It is clear that YHWH does not want to punish his people; rather, he wants them to return to him. Should the people respond to the call to repent, the fate of the other nations will not befall them. Although the nations had been cut off, they will not be cut off, nor will they suffer any punishment. However, the opposite has happened. They are eager to continue in their corrupt behaviour, as is pointed out to them in verses 1–4.

8. Verse 8 is the culmination of this unit. It is introduced by a prominent *Therefore* which draws the conclusion to the prophecy uttered thus far. Verse 8 is also introduced by the important and solemn phrase *declares the LORD* as another indication that a final conclusion will now be drawn. The people, and in particular those living in Jerusalem, are called upon to *wait* upon YHWH. They are assured that a day will come when YHWH will rise to *testify*. The return of the theme of the Day of YHWH is important. The coming day will be a day of universal judgment when the nations together with the people of God will be judged.

After the accusations levelled at the people and the city of Jerusalem, one expects a prophecy of judgment on God's people. Quite unexpectedly the *nations* will be gathered and YHWH's *wrath* and *anger* will be poured out on them. In the light of the previous verses the disturbing news is that Jerusalem and the people of God will be part of the universal judgment pronounced here. There will be no difference between YHWH's people and the other nations: they will all suffer the same judgment. The last part of verse 8 is virtually a repetition of what was already stated in 1:18 and the theme of a universal judgment is a return to the opening verses of the book in 1:2–3. Is it possible that verse 8 allows for a glimmer of hope that judgment may be averted because the people are called upon to wait for YHWH?

Meaning
Where the people of the Lord refuse to listen to the voice of God, disregard God's instructions to correct sinful behaviour, do not trust him and are not interested in seeking his presence in worship, they become rebellious, defiled and oppressive. When the relationship with God is neglected, it then leads to a decay in relationships with others. The four groups of people mentioned in verses 3–4 are those who are supposed to render service to the ordinary people of the city and, by extension, the country. Those who are in what we would today call government administration are servants of the people and consequently ought not to be perceived as predators to

be feared by society. Religious leaders also should act in society in such a way that they can be trusted for what they proclaim and do. The prophet speaks out against the whole of society. Both civil and religious leaders come under his scrutiny.

Yet, in spite of all the injustices that can be seen in society, YHWH is present as the just and righteous God dispensing his justice day by day. Where people have to suffer injustice, it is often their faith in the righteous God within their midst that keeps them going. It is sad when the conduct of believers is no different from that of non-believers. This is what is implied in this unit. It is therefore even more disturbing that the same fate will befall non-believers and believers. Prophecies regarding a worldwide judgment on foreign nations are also found elsewhere in the prophetic literature (Ezek. 38:4, 8, 14; Joel 3:2; Zech. 12:3).

ii. Salvation announced to the nations (3:9–13)

Context

With verse 9 a startling new turn of events is announced. Instead of final judgment and punishment to the point of total annihilation of nations, kingdoms and in fact the whole world, a completely new possibility is foreseen.

Comment

9–10. In the previous units the foreign nations were addressed. It was YHWH who announced doom and destruction upon them. Now the very same nations are addressed again but this time with an announcement of salvation. Once again it is YHWH who will take the initiative in this new possibility of redemption rather than judgment. He will transform the speech of the nations to a pure speech. The verb rendered by NIV as *purify* (or to 'change' or 'overturn') is significant as in other contexts it is used to announce judgment (Gen. 19:25; Jer. 20:16; Amos 4:11). Instead of an announcement of judgment, however, a prophecy of salvation is proclaimed. The language of the nations will be changed so that they will now call upon the name of YHWH. YHWH alone will be worshipped in prayer and praise and in this way all nations will honour the first commandment of the Decalogue. Some scholars (Nogalski 2011: 743–744; Motyer 1998: 951) have seen the reversal of

Genesis 11:1–9 in this unit: at the tower of Babel the confusion of speech caused disunity, but now the language of the nations will be changed to unite people in their worship and service of God.

To *call on the name of* YHWH means to worship him in prayer in formal religious ceremonies at the temple and to plead for his help in times of distress. This new initiative will not be restricted to the cultic sphere of life; YHWH will be served in all aspects of ordinary life. All nations will live according to God's will. Moreover, it will be done 'with one shoulder' (NIV *shoulder to shoulder*), an idiomatic expression drawn from animals being yoked together in a common task. It denotes people serving YHWH together in a remarkable unity.

Even people as far away as the region *beyond the rivers of Cush* (Ethiopia) on the African continent will be included in this new time of grace and salvation (2:12). People who worship God will also *bring [him] offerings*. The vision of the prophet is still a universal one in which people of foreign nations will come and worship and bring or send sacrifices to honour YHWH. This is in line with other parts of the prophetic literature where a pilgrimage of people from the nations to Jerusalem/Zion is foreseen (Isa. 2:3; Jer. 31:6; Mic. 4:1–4; Zech. 14:16). It is unlikely that the people of God in diaspora is meant here, for that would be in direct contradiction to verse 9.

11–13. With verse 11 the focus of attention shifts back to Jerusalem again (cf. 3:1–8). On the day (3:8) that will come in the future, Jerusalem will not have to feel ashamed for its deeds of the past. Those deeds were named in the previous unit in no uncertain terms and are now summarized by pointing out the people who are *arrogant boasters*. Previously (2:3), the people were admonished to *Seek righteousness, seek humility*, but here the exact opposite of that attitude among the people is described. People have acted with pride and haughtiness in the past. Pride and haughtiness can thus be seen as a summary of the sins mentioned in the previous unit (3:1–8). To be rebellious and disobedient, to refuse to accept correction, to act with arrogance and to do violence to the Torah are all manifestations of an attitude of indifference to YHWH that can be summarized as human pride. This situation will, however, change, for the guilty people will be removed from the city. Instead of being *haughty* the people will now be *humble*. For the first and only time in the book Mount Zion is named as *my holy hill*. The holy God can only be worshipped on his holy mountain by his holy people. Being *meek and humble* is the opposite of being proud and haughty. In contrast to those of whom it is explicitly said that they do not trust in YHWH (3:2), it is the meek and humble who put their trust *in the name of* YHWH. The terms translated *meek and humble* can also be understood as referring to the poor, dependent, weak and vulnerable in society. It is the *remnant* who are characterized as *meek and humble* and as those who submit themselves to YHWH because they have realized it is best to put their trust in him. To *trust* in God means to take refuge in YHWH as he is ultimately the One who will protect those who are vulnerable.

With three short sentences the way of life of the righteous remnant of Israel is then described. In the first place, just as YHWH does no wrong (3:5), so *They will do no wrong*. They will act in the same way that YHWH acts. Second, *they will tell no lies*. To speak the truth is a hallmark of true believers. Third, they will not be *deceitful* in any way. Just as the speech of the peoples will be purified (3:9), so the *mouths* of the righteous remnant will not be guilty of deceit.

The last part of verse 13 paints a pastoral scene of bliss and peace. Like a flock of sheep lying down with enough to feed on and with no fear of an attack of any kind, the new restored remnant will enjoy the blessing of restfulness and enduring peace (Lev. 26:6; Jer. 30:10; Ezek. 34:28; Mic. 4:4). This picture is in stark contrast to the situation portrayed earlier (3:3), where the leaders in society were described as predators.

Meaning

YHWH is indeed the universal God. He created everything and he has power over all of creation, including all the nations of the earth. His universal rule is shown not only in pronouncing judgment upon all nations (including his own people), but also in announcing salvation to all people. If the region *beyond the rivers of Cush* is reached then the whole known world has been reached. True adherence to God is shown by sincere worship and serving him in everything one does in life. The remnant is the group of people who submit to YHWH in a spirit of meekness and humility. They know that one has to realize one's dependence on God for our very existence and therefore take refuge in him instead of in one's own strength. This attitude is exactly the opposite of the kind of behaviour described in the previous unit (3:1–8). The way in which believers conduct themselves in society is also important. Like YHWH who does no wrong, it is expected from the remnant to do no wrong. It is interesting that not speaking lies is mentioned here. We live in a world today where the boundaries between truth and blatant lies have become vague, hence the new terms 'post-truth' and 'fake news'. In this kind of world, the word of God in Zephaniah is apt: 'they will utter no lies' (NRSV). Believers may expect the blessing of God by which he will take care of them by providing for their needs and granting them peace.

Thus, as in so many other places in the Old Testament, God's mercy trumps his wrath time and again.

iii. A call to joy because God is with his people (3:14–20)
Context
The last unit of the book commences with a call to sing and rejoice. Nogalski (2011: 748) detected a chiastic structure in 3:14–17: (A) Rejoice Zion, YHWH has withdrawn judgment (3:14–15a); (B) King YHWH is in your midst (3:15bα); (C) Do not fear, Zion (3:15bβ); (C') 'Do not fear!' Jerusalem will be told (3:16); (B') Warrior YHWH is in your midst (3:17a); (A') YHWH will rejoice over you, Zion (3:17b). The chiastic structure of verses 14–17 distinguishes them from verses 18–20 so that 3:14–20 is made up of two sub-units. Motyer (1998: 956) proposed a similar structure: (A) the joy of Zion over the Lord (v. 14); (B) the Lord's action in deliverance (v. 15a–b); (C) the Lord, the indwelling king (v. 15c); (D) the city without fear (vv. 15d–16); (C') the Lord, the indwelling God (v. 17a); (B') the Lord's action in salvation (v. 17b); (A') the joy of the Lord over Zion (v. 17c–e).

Comment
14. Verse 14 is characterized by four imperative verbs (*sing, shout, rejoice*, 'exult' [NRSV]) and three vocatives (*Daughter Zion, Israel, Daughter Jerusalem*). This call made to Jerusalem is in stark contrast to the description of the city in 3:1. The verbs used call for joyous and noisy jubilation. Calling the people of God *Daughter Zion, Israel*

and *Daughter Jerusalem* signifies a restored covenant relationship between YHWH and his people.

15. Verse 15 provides the reason for the call to joy. The judgments of the past mentioned in 3:1–8 have been done away with. The proof of that is that no *enemy* will pose a threat to the people any more.

The second, related promise made to the remnant is that YHWH, as the *King of Israel*, will be present with them. The metaphor of YHWH as king is an important motif in the Old Testament (Deut. 33:5; 1 Sam. 12:12; Isa. 43:15; 44:6; Mal. 1:14; and often in the Psalms). YHWH is portrayed as the supreme ruler and, as with a good king, all his actions will be to the benefit of his people. The emphasis on YHWH's presence is equally important. YHWH's presence was one of the main motifs during the exodus from Egypt. According to Exodus 13:21–22 YHWH went ahead of the people in a pillar of cloud by day and in a pillar of fire by night. In fact, the name of YHWH revealed to Moses in Exodus 3 suggests that he is and will be the ever-present God. The consequence of YHWH's presence in the midst of his people is that they will be safe from any *harm* and will have nothing to *fear*. Earlier the inhabitants of Jerusalem were of the opinion that YHWH was inactive and *will do nothing, either good or bad* (1:12). The situation has changed dramatically in that there will now be no doubt in the minds of the rescued remnant that he is indeed present as the King of Israel. YHWH's presence in the midst of his people is a reiteration of what was said already in 3:5.

16. Verse 16 is a repetition of the assurance given in 3:15 that there will be no reason to fear any harm in the coming undefined future dispensation. With YHWH as the King of Israel who is in their midst, there is no reason for fear. *On that day* is a reminder of what was said earlier (3:11) when the emphasis was on the judgment to be executed. Here the emphasis is on the end result of what will happen in the future. The assurance of YHWH's presence together with his promise of protection must also act as an encouragement to the people not to lose hope and determination.

17. Once again, the people are assured of YHWH's presence. He is portrayed as a mighty God ready to deliver them. The depiction of God as a *Mighty Warrior* is not an unfamiliar way in the Old Testament of conveying the message that he is the one who will

help his people in their distress (Isa. 42:13; Jer. 20:11). Over against
the harsh words of judgment, YHWH is also the God who *take[s]
great delight in* his people. It is not at once clear what the meaning
of the next line in verse 17 is. It is noteworthy that YHWH's *love*
for his people is expressed with the same verb used to describe the
love Jacob had for Rachel (Gen. 29:20) and Michal had for David
(1 Sam. 18:20, 28). The more difficult part is how to interpret
YHWH's 'silence' in his love for his people (see NRSV margin). The
explanation by Ben Zvi (1991: 249–252) is the most convincing.
According to him, in numerous instances in the Old Testament the
verb used conveys the meaning of 'refraining from reacting to
the deeds of someone else' (Ben Zvi 1991: 251). Hence verse 17
wants to communicate the message that 'God will refrain from
executing the judgment because of love for the people' (Ben Zvi
1991: 252). Verse 17 concludes with the remarkable statement that
YHWH will *rejoice over* his people *with singing*. This sub-unit started
with a call to the remnant to sing, and quite significantly it comes
to an end with YHWH singing, with the same verb used in both
cases.

18. Verse 18 is difficult to translate in a way that makes sense,
but the main thrust nevertheless seems clear. In the light of the
previous verses, where the relationship between YHWH and his
people has been restored and is a cause for joy, there is no room for
sorrow during *festivals*. In a situation where the people may experience the presence of YHWH, where their punishment has been
taken away and where they may now enjoy peace without a hint of
fear, there is no place for *reproach*. Instead, the people are reassured
of God's love for them. Oppressors will no longer pose a threat as
God himself will deal with them.

19–20. In the Hebrew text verse 19 starts with an exclamation
(*hinĕnî*) usually translated as 'Behold' (RSV) or 'Look out!' Once
again, God's intervention on behalf of his people is reiterated. In
particular the people will be liberated from oppression. YHWH is
the warrior who will act decisively. The verse forms a nice chiastic
structure: (A) no more oppressors (v. 19a–b); (B) the personally
helpless saved (v. 19c); (B′) the personally banished gathered
(v. 19d); (A′) no more shame, only praise universally (v. 19e–f)
(Motyer 1998: 961). In the second part of the verse the metaphor of

YHWH as a warrior is changed to YHWH as a shepherd who will tend his people as a shepherd looks after his flock of sheep. The *lame* being saved refers, then, more to injured sheep than to the physical disabilities of people. Nothing, not even personal or physical difficulties, will prevent YHWH restoring his people. Just as an injured sheep is unable to help itself, so the lame are those unable to rescue themselves. Only God can and will bring a change in their dire circumstances. The people will be brought together, reunited as the one people of God. They will be restored to *praise and honour* among the nations. The same thought is repeated in verse 20. The *honour* shown them by the nations refers to their name being restored: they will have a good reputation as a people whose *fortunes* have been restored. Restoration to glory among the nations will follow their current humiliation, and the other nations will be witnesses to this redemptive event. There are no direct historical allusions in verses 18–20 but the situation reflected is an exilic one.

The book that commenced with a universal vision of total and inevitable destruction thus concludes on a hopeful note. There will be no total destruction but rather a glorious restoration of the people.

Meaning

This unit presents us with a remarkable statement of God's love despite the sins of his people. Time and again, God puts the sins and guilt of his people behind him and is willing to restore their broken relationship with him. The result of a restored relationship with God is joy and jubilation, and a commitment once again to be a servant of the King and to experience his guidance and protection so that believers can live without fear of harm. Fear makes one weak, but where there is no fear there is no reason to despair; rather, one can act courageously in the service of YHWH, the King of Israel.

There is an interesting contrast created in chapter 3. Those living in Jerusalem are accused of not fearing YHWH, which will result in doom and judgment (3:7–8). In 3:15–16, however, the remnant are assured that there will be no need to fear external threats. Thus, not to fear YHWH makes one fearful of the future because of the coming judgment, but to fear YHWH means to live without fear.

God's grace trumps his judgment once again in the book of Zephaniah. Instead of devastation for the whole of creation, God will take the initiative and restore his people from exile and reunite them in the land in such a way that the other nations will witness it. When that happens, the people's name and reputation will also be restored among the nations. There is thus a clear movement in the book from judgment to salvation, from destruction to restoration. The book finally concludes with a solemn declaration that what has been uttered here is what YHWH says. In this way, the book comes to an end by forming an *inclusio*, having started with the 'word of YHWH' in 1:1.

Finding the Textbook You Need

The IVP Academic Textbook Selector
is an online tool for instantly finding the IVP books
suitable for over 250 courses across 24 disciplines.

----

ivpacademic.com